The Cheater's Handbook

The Naughty Student's Bible

Bob Corbett

ReganBooks
An Imprint of HarperCollins*Publishers*

HarperCollins books may be purchased for educational, business, or sales promotional use. For information please write: Special Markets Department, HarperCollins Publishers, Inc., 10 East 53rd Street, New York, NY 10022.

FIRST EDITION

Designed by Laura Lindgren

Illustrated by Glen Fairchild
Figures 7-11, 7-12, 7-13, and 7-14 by Bob Corbett

ISBN 0-06-098812-6

98 99 00 01 02 10 9 8 7 6 5 4 3 2 1

"It is as impossible for a man to be cheated by anyone but himself, as for a thing to be, and not to be, at the same time."

—RALPH WALDO EMERSON
Essays (First Series), "Self-Reliance"

"So this Jefferson dude was like, 'Look, the reason we left this England place is 'cause it was so bogus, so if we don't get some primo rules ourselves—pronto—then we're just gonna be bogus, too."

—JEFF SPICCOLI
Fast Times at Ridgemont High

I would actually like to dedicate this book to a teacher. During the 11th grade "writing semester" at Hopkins, Mr. Bucar did such a wonderfully *engaging* job that he destroyed any shred of desire I may have ever had to cheat in English thereafter (though I was pretty damn tempted with that silly *Canterbury Tales* memorization for What's-Her-Face). As a result, I pursue the glory of the written word with all my vigor. If all teachers brought such passionate energy to their classrooms, perhaps this book would become obsolete. But, until then . . .

CONTENTS

INTRODUCTION

There are probably two types of people who are going to read this book: students and teachers.

On one hand, you have the lackluster scholastic endeavorer who knows his stuff. No, not his academic stuff—his own stuff. He knows that his ass'll be too lazy to get around to an assignment every now and then and that when that life-threatening moment arrives, he'll have *The Cheater's Handbook* in hand to make sure he's doing his corner-cutting right, to make sure that he is indeed taking the shortest path from Point F to Point A. (The expected societal analysis about why he feels the need to accomplish this can be found in the final chapter.) Yes, *The Cheater's Handbook* will be the one book in his life that he ever does study.

On the other hand, you have the teacher who somehow discovered this manual and thought he'd get one up on all those miserable little cretins who turn his life into a winless *Tom & Jerry*-esque combat day in and day out. To that breed of academic, let us first say: You're doing something terribly wrong. Very rarely does a great teacher have a room full of cheaters. A truly great teacher can take even a compulsive cheater—one who thrives on it not out of necessity but for sport—and transform him for that one semester into an eager beaver who shows up early, enjoys doing the homework, and comes to ask questions on his own time. How? By making it interesting! When are all you teachers out there going to realize how boring you make *every* thing you talk about? Do you think that paraphrasing the previous night's reading assignment is a creative way to teach?

No, of course you don't. But that's all most of you do. So either you really are *incapable* of creativity (which no one is) or, even worse, you really are your worst fear: *too lazy to cut it in the real world.* Someone who shuns the traditional workforce in favor of merely paraphrasing the textbook they are assigned to teach is indeed hiding from the real world, clearly dwelling in the same echelon as the proverbial "bump on a log." However, an individual who shuns the traditional workforce and proactively shapes the minds of tomorrow's adults by bringing knowledge alive to them *is* cutting it in the real world. Yes, they may have short hours and summer vacations, but they are making a massive positive impact on society.

With that said, we posit to all of you teachers reading this: Which category are you going to allow yourself to stand in? The avoider of the real world or the impacter on the real world? It really is up to you. But if you have chosen the latter, be forewarned that if you have recurrent cheating problems in your classes, you are failing. For no great teacher—those teachers who can make ancient wars and chemical processes and anything else *come alive*—need refer to this book. Moreover, any teacher who does consult this book for anything other than innocent entertainment leads a failed life. Catching students cheating is not the solution. *Negating their desire to cheat is the solution.* It's the same as with anything else. For instance, putting more police on the streets is not the solution to rampant crime; that only leads to a police state. Rebuilding the family is the solution (or at least half of it). Alright, you get the point. Now go figure out how to do it. Go watch some inspirational movies, go read some sappy book, or Christ—drink twice as much caffeine before class!

Now, introduction-wise, let us cover some points of interest before we whirlwind you into the world of cheating. Since we're probably not dealing with the finest attention spans on Earth here, we might as well start bulleting this introduction up into convenient little fragments like we do with the rest of the book. Here are the points of interest:

☑ **Disclaimer**: As we will reiterate several times through this little tome, *WE ARE NOT BY ANY MEANS AGAINST LEARNING ITSELF. NO. WE JUST KNOW THAT A LOT OF TIMES IT SIMPLY FAILS TO HAPPEN FOR ONE REASON OR ANOTHER AND THAT YOU DON'T WANT TO SUFFER THE POOR GRADES THAT YOU ULTIMATELY DESERVE.*

☑ **Qualification to Write This Book:** The author has been an avid scholastic cheater since the fifth grade, when he quit the Gifted & Talented program in favor of being a slapdick. Over the next ten years he would thrive on cheating like a sport, nay, a passion—the excitement and free time it gave him was exhilarating, and that exhilaration was addictive. Now, though, unfortunately, he has to resort to writing books like this to make money. In other words, he doesn't recommend following his path. Study!

☑ **Vernacular:** Two words we will be using a lot are "neighbor" and "they." "Neighbor" we use just because it's a funny reminder of being in class ("eyes off your neighbor's paper!"). We would never use it, of course, except to poke fun at it.

The word "they," however, will repeatedly be used incorrectly. Yes, we know that when the pronoun is ambiguous, one should use the phrase "he or she," as in "when he or she corrects your test . . ." Sorry, though, that's just too cumbersome for us. People generally don't say that crap in day-to-day speech either. They say "they." So don't waste your time writing us about trivial grammatical discrepancies. A movement for the acceptance of "They" as a singular pronoun is now underway, people, so stand back!

We, or I, will also be wavering between using "we" or "I", so just deal with it. There is a method to the madness, but don't try to figure it out.

☑ **Imminent Sequel:** Yes, already in the works is the sequel: *The Cheater's Handbook's Extra Credit: Ideas From Our Readers*. We know that we cannot have possibly gathered together every great cheating tactic in this compendium, so send on in your ideas and cheating stories. Your name (or pseudonym of your choice) will get full credit right under the idea or story!

☑ **One More Thing:** To all you tattle-tales: Before you go off and tell on someone for cheating, consider this: You are not a role-model student. The only reason someone tells on someone else for cheating is because that person doesn't like the fact that the cheater is getting as many points as they are for all their hard work. Therefore, you are just as coldly ensconced in this never-ending rat race for numbers (see

Chapter 14) as the cheater is. A true student would be completely satisfied in the knowledge that the cheaters will invariably suffer later in life as a result of all the knowledge they never learned. A true student is concerned with knowledge, not points.

Chapter 1

Getting the Right Juice

We don't want to shatter any high hopes you may have had about ten minutes and twelve bucks ago, but this handbook is not some kind of magic scroll that will enable you to do absolutely nothing and then walk out of the classroom with straight A's. No. Proper cheating is hard work. Of course, it's not one one-hundredth as hard as actually learning all that stuff the teacher's always talking about that you probably figure you'll just forget anyway (. . . so why listen?) but cheating still demands a good amount of time and preparation. Even the greatest of us cheaters have been known to kick ourselves in the wee hours before a test because we can no longer ignore the grim reality that we have nothing to even so much as scrawl down on our off-hand palm.

So blow the dust off your syllabus and actually look at it, and begin scheming at least a day before the dreaded test. In the next chapter, we move into cheat-sheets. And if you don't have anything besides the textbook from which to make a good one, you'll be sorrier than an impotent man on a free trip to Mustang Ranch. There are two things which, when combined properly, can make cracking that heavy textbook or even bringing it home unnecessary. There's also a third thing that's even better, but next to impossible to come by.

NOTES (AND HANDOUTS)

Alright, chances are that if you bought this book, taking notes is about as much a part of your daily life as waking up an extra hour early for that morning jog—it just doesn't really happen, though you wish it would. But that's nothing to be ashamed of. Taking notes is a pain in the butt, and if a roomful of people are all writing down the same thing, why should you waste your valuable, limited attention span on writing all that stuff down too? Surely *someone* who has taken good notes and kept track of the key handouts will be kind enough to let you "check them out." And whether or not they know that this means you'll run off to furiously photocopy their semester's blood, sweat, and tears depends on your relationship with them and/or how cool they are. Here are the four basic breeds of "friends" from whom you can "borrow" notes:

The Admirer

Score. You're set. Look no further. If there's a good note-taker in your class who just happens to have a crush on you, "like" you, or even just make the occasional "googly eyes" toward you, exploit them for every note and handout they're worth. This may sound a little harsh, but hey, that's how life works. Have you ever seen a drop-dead gorgeous woman driving around in a really crappy pile-of-junk car? No, and if they didn't earn whatever they do have through their own merit, you can bet your booty that some putz somewhere got taken advantage of, whether he admits it or not and even *cares* or not. It's the same principle here, only on a smaller scale. Walk up to your prey, flash that winning smile, and sweet-talk their notes out of them. Don't be too obvious about it, though. Try to talk to them a bit a few days before the test. Wait a second: If any of this— the oldest schmooz principle on Earth—actually needs explaining to you at this point in your life, then it probably isn't even an option for you in the first place. Then again, there's a first time for everything. . . .

The Buddy

If your would-be co-conspirator is a good friend of yours, then you should likewise have no problem getting the notes. But perhaps you should ask yourself first, "Wait, how good could the notes be if this person's a friend of *mine*?" Something is better than nothing, of course, but don't settle for four pages of doodling just because it—unlike your doodling—has three poorly defined terms mired in it somewhere.

"That Guy," or, "That Chick"
If your mark isn't a good friend of yours, be tactical. Ask nicely first, lying if necessary. (Say that all your notes got soaking wet or something.) If asking nicely doesn't work, offer to do some kind of favor in return, preferably one that involves aiding them on future tests. ("I swear I can get the final, dude. I swear."). If promising favors doesn't do the trick, you're obviously dealing with some kind of prick here. But if you've already gone this far, then they're clearly your only hope for quality notes, so offer a little cash or something. Remember, teachers *always* pull out stuff from the notes on tests, if for no other reason than to justify their existence (i.e., to remind themselves that you couldn't just as easily have read the textbook and learned the entire course on your own). Getting the notes and handouts is essential, no matter what lengths you must go to. *How else will you know what to put on your cheatsheet?*

The Local Merlin
Many colleges have a nearby academic guru who knows basically everything or can skim through the material and break it down into a sheet of layman's terms for you in a matter of minutes. If the stuff is too thick for you to even know where to begin, chip in with a couple of classmates for an hour with such a

guru. An hour with one of these brainiacs usually runs about seventy bucks or so.

(*TIP*: Actually, the best thing to do is lay low, let other people dish out their cash to this educational extortionist, and then later on play dumb and ask to photocopy "Uh, whatever you guys have. . . Yeah, this looks cool," not letting on that you know they just spent their weekend's partying money on it.)

OLD TESTS

Tests from previous years are a must, especially in college. And the best part? Studying them is legal! Even if a teacher changes their test every semester, old tests still show you what *kind* of things they look for, what *kind* of questions they ask; e.g., if an old psychology question goes "Which of the following substances is the *most* addictive," then you can expect the new one to maybe go "Which of the following substances is *least* addictive?" Figuring out what topics the teacher likes makes it a lot easier to pick the right things from your notes to put on your cheatsheet.

Of course, if you can get a series of past tests and find certain questions that show up throughout them, you can expect those questions on your test and then simply memorize the answer. (Or, if you *must*, put the answer on your cheatsheet—but come on now, people.)

If the teacher is actually so much of a lazy drunk that they do in fact use the same exact questions every year, then obviously you're set. But be careful about just simply memorizing multiple–choice answers in your head by rote, like "A-B-A-C-A-B . . ." As drunk and lazy as the teacher may be, they might at least change the order of the questions. It's wiser to either learn (or write on your cheatsheet) two key words for each problem—one from the question and one from the correct answer.

Where To Get Them

Old tests are a lot easier to get your paws on when you're in college than they were in high school. Most fraternity and sorority houses have some kind of "scholar's office" or some other fancily named file cabinet full of old tests. Don't go straight to the dorkier houses, though. Think about it. It's probably the *less* academically oriented houses that keep the best files.

The best way to get old tests, though, takes a little foresight. If you know what classes you'll be taking next semester, ask someone who's taking the course *now* to save all of their stuff for you. This is easier than getting the notes of someone you're taking a class with now, because:

A. They won't need those notes anymore.

B. They can't bitch that you never go to class and are taking advantage of them.

This, unfortunately, is also pretty much the only way to get old tests in high school, since test files usually aren't available.

THE TEST

Ah, the coup de tests. The ultimate score. *The* test. Yes, and unless you've got a serious inside source, don't expect to see too many of these—if any—in your lifetime. And unless that one diamond in the rough virtually falls into your lap, don't waste your time and jeopardize your future by actively hunting for a copy of the actual test your class is going to be taking. Most teachers don't even create the test until the night before; those who do make them earlier than that rarely leave a copy lying around anywhere that you could possibly get your hands on it. That is, where you could get it, photocopy it, and return it unnoticed. Right. The odds are overwhelmingly against you, and the possible lifetime consequences far outweigh the specter of getting one fleeting A.

Your best hope is to befriend or seduce the teacher's assistant. But, judging by the way a lot of those characters look, it's probably not even worth that.

Another dim hope is that there will be botched copies left in the trash bin next to the faculty photocopy machine, but there's always a teacher or two somewhere in the vicinity sucking down coffee. And their interest is certainly going to piqued by seeing a slapdick like you nosing around their little cigarette sanctuary.

Basically, an original test has to fall into your lap. Things like that usually only happen when you least expect it—so just don't think about it, and you might have a chance. See Chapter 12, "Legends of the Mall," for a good story about getting the test.

Score!

If by some miracle you do in fact score an actual copy of the upcoming test, don't tell anyone. Your phone will be ringing off the hook and your door'll be broken down. If you just can't help sharing a good thing, at least rip off a page or change some questions or something. You can *not* have five to ten people getting an A+ or 100 on the same test that you are going to get your first A+ or 100 on. Not only does it imbalance the curve, but it looks bad; the teacher will know something's up.

On the other side of the glass, if you get the test from a friend who got it from a friend who got it from a friend, and so on, keep in mind that the original source may have known the principle in the paragraph above and altered the test so that moochers like you wouldn't get a hundred too. In other words, don't think that just because you got a copy of the test that you're set. Check it out. Verify the answers. And for God's sake, memorize it. This is no time to double your chances of getting caught by using a cheatsheet.

Chapter 2

Making the Sheets of Life

Cheatsheets (also known as "crib notes"—but that's just a little too 1950s, *Leave It To Beaver* for our taste) are the lifeblood of any underprepared test-taker and can take on many different forms, be it an overstressed law student's micro-copied U.S. Constitution or just right-of-way arrows drawn on the wrist of some zit-faced kid taking the driving exam. Whether on your skin, on a scrap of paper, in your calculator, or on a typed-and-miniaturized "masterpiece" from Kinko's, you absolutely *must* bring some kind of cheatsheet to any test.

This is not even to say you must *use* a cheatsheet, but that you must at the very least *bring* one for insurance, for that much needed sense of security. Think about jumping out of an airplane. No matter how sure you felt that the first parachute was well-prepared and ready to work, would you even think of taking the plunge without the backup chute packed? Of course not. You should have the same mentality with cheating. No matter how well you think you know the material, no matter how many hours on end you study, always, always, *always* bring something written down that you can refer to in a moment of panic, when your mind goes blank. The main reason we stress this so much is that just having something up your sleeve (pun intended) often greatly decreases your chances of actually panicking and needing it.

Back to the corny parachute analogy: Don't you think you'd have an easier time opening the first chute smoothly and successfully if your life didn't *absolutely* depend on your doing so? Okay, okay, you get it.

Anyway, another reason you should always make a cheatsheet is that quite often something miraculous can happen when doing so: You actually *learn* the material! There's nothing sweeter than that surprising feeling during a test of "Hey, wait a minute, I actually know this stuff—screw cheating!"

Remember, this handbook is strictly cheating-oriented and does not purport to teach any learning efficiency methods. There are many instructors out there who are far more qualified to teach such methods, and many (boring) books written by these experts.

But as any one of those books will likely tell you, one way to learn information is to simply copy it down on a sheet of paper. (Of course, they probably don't have a 2" × 2" scrap in mind). So go ahead and always make a cheatsheet, if for no other reason than you might actually learn something, which would be best of all. Remember, we are not by any means against learning itself. No. We just know that, for one reason or another, a lot of times it simply just does not happen, and you don't want to get the bad grades you ultimately deserve. Who would? It's like, if you hadn't exercised all year, but suddenly the day before you hit the beach for spring break there was a way to get an incredible body overnight that didn't really *harm* you, would you pass it up? No way! (Of course, if one took this analogy all the way, you would bring the hottest babe there back to your pad but then ultimately be unable to *perform*, if you know what we mean.)

Here are various shapes and forms cheatsheets can take, and the pro's and cons of each:

THE CLASSIC

The chances that any of you reading this have never used the ol' Classic cheatsheet shown in Figure 2-1 are probably about the same as the chances that you have never used the answers in the back of your math book to breeze through a homework assignment. *Everyone uses them.*

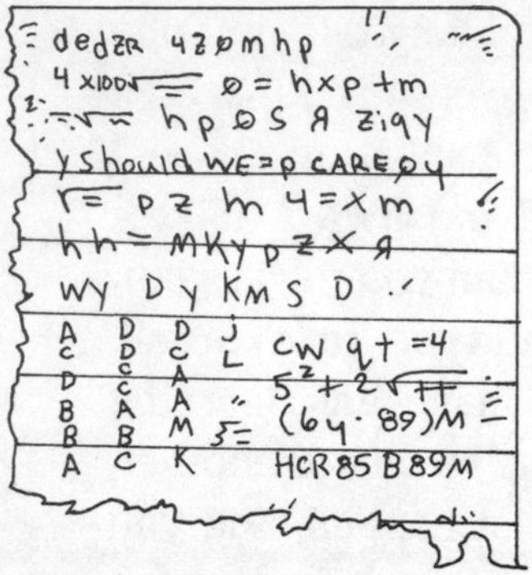

```
= dedza 42pmhp
4 xiDor = p = hxp +m
-=~= hp @S A ziqy
y should WE=p CAREpy
r= p z m 4=x m
hh= mKy p z x A
wy Dy Km S D
A  D  D  J   cw  q+ =4
c  p  c  L   5² +2(+++
D  c  A
B  A  M  5= (64·89)M
R  B
A  c  K   HCR85 B89M
```

Figure 2-1

You knowww… About an hour before test time, you just rip off the top left square of a piece of notebook paper, sharpen your pencil to maximum pointiness, and start squeezing volumes of information onto both sides of this $2'' \times 2''$ phenomenon, wondering if *The Guinness Book of Records* has a category for the world's smallest legible writing.

The Classic is a very strong model. It's easy to make and, if spotted by the teacher, easy to eat (like it's a stick of chewing gum, of course). Whether you want lead or ink going into your digestive system is up to you, but it's usually better to make cheatsheets with pencil because you can erase and fix them, and lead writing doesn't bleed through to the other side like ink can. Ink can also smudge under the sweat from your palm. Other than that, the only real problem you can run into with one of these babies is that the small writing you were so proud of when you made it might be really hard to decipher under test conditions. It takes a few runs with the Classic before you get your own personal "Amount of Info divided by Space times Legibility" formula right. Just remember: Never make the cheatsheet bigger than a Wrigley's gum wrapper, unless the teacher is just *completely* oblivious. In that case, use a full sheet of paper. Go to town!

Whatever the size, abbreviate, abbreviate, abbreviate! Don't consume space writing out entire definitions. Just write the key words next to the term, which should be abbreviated itself. Remember, spelling rarely—if ever—counts on tests other than spelling tests.

DOUBLE CLASSIC DELUXE

Once you've mastered the Classic and if your classroom situation allows you enough mobility (i.e., if the teacher can't see), you may want to try out the Double Classic Deluxe (Figure 2-2). This two all-beef patty special sauce lettuce cheese bad boy is simply a "4 × 2" Classic folded in half, packing twice the dates, formulas, whatever. You've got to use pencil, though, or else the side folded inward will smudge against itself.

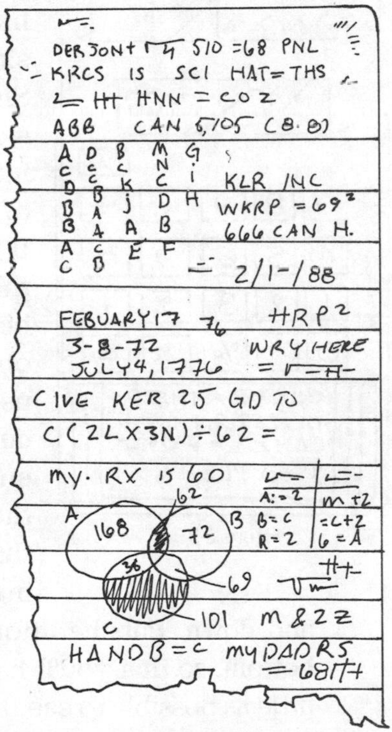

Of course, you could make even more multi-sided cheatsheets, but all the folding and unfolding involved in using

Figure 2-2

those makes noise and is just asking for trouble. Don't get any more fancy than the Double Classic Deluxe. If anything, it's better to just get bigger than more complicated, like a straight 4" × 4" Classic.

SHEATH SHEET

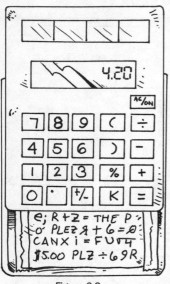

Figure 2-3

Try saying *that* five times in a row really fast and you'll sound like an immigrant taxicab driver skidding into an accident. The Sheath Sheet is just a big one-sided Classic that fits perfectly into the sliding protective sheath of your calculator (Figure 2-3). If you don't have a calculator like this, *get one*. This is one of the best cheatsheet methods there is; obviously, though, it can only be used in classes that involve calculators, such as math and science classes. Make sure to tape the sheet down to the sheath so that it is not damaged when sliding the calculator strategically up and down. Put the information you need most at the bottom, so that you'll have to slide the sheath open as little as possible to see the goods.

CYBERPUNK

Okay, maybe technically that term has nothing to do with this tactic, but it's just such a stupid, silly word we're going to use it anyway. All we're talking about here is something any of you with the right equipment has surely stumbled upon already. Any of you with one of those daddy calculator/life organizer thingies can simply program all the information in the world in there and leave it under some hidden codename or something (Figure 2-4). The teacher thinks you're just using the calculator part, but of course you're busy scrolling through sixty-seven different formulas and scientific laws, you dirty, low-down, no-good *cyberpunk*.

Figure 2-4

Figure 2-5

THE SO-CALLED "MASTERPIECE"

The typed, shrunken down, professional-looking "Masterpiece" (Figure 2-5) is, of course, the ultimate cheatsheet for those of you who have the time and skill. Most of you don't, though, which is the reason we have surrounded this one with quotation marks and don't really take it all that seriously. These must be made the night before, and for most tests, anyone who puts that much foresight into a cheatsheet is a fool. Cheatsheets shouldn't be made until an hour before the test at the earliest. This makes for the most efficient cheatsheets, since then you can just put down *the remaining information that you have not yet learned by then*. Making the sheet a whole twenty-four hours in advance on your home computer, you're liable to waste valuable space with an easy piece of info that you'll find you will have completely learned by the next morning.

Also, such premeditation means doom if the teacher snags one of these. It shows them that you didn't even *attempt* to study the night before, but rather spent an hour and half figuring out how to use your computer as something other than the $2,000 video-game player and Internet-porn surfer that it usually is. On that same note, do not *ever* laminate one of these, unless you want to run the risk of having that big chunk of plastic gyrating around your digestive system longer than that beef jerky that's been in there since third grade. Keep in mind the *Golden Rule of Getting Caught* with a cheatsheet, as discussed in Chapter 8, "BUSTED!!!": *YOU MUST ALWAYS EAT THE EVIDENCE*.

The only time you should really micro-type a cheatsheet like this is when there's tons of impossible-to-remember formulas or dates or something, and you just cannot possibly handwrite them all legibly. Other than that, you're better off spending your time the night before scrambling around getting old tests and notes and maybe even studying them to boot. (Wishful thinking never hurts.)

BAG O' TRICKS

Here's an easy but not so great one: You can just write some key stuff on your bookbag (providing it's light-colored). What's not so great about this one is that you can pretty much only do it once; furthermore, it ruins your bag, and it's a pain in the rear to get anything legible on there in the first place.

On the bag, however, you can rest your notebook, the manila back of which can be filled out from top to bottom with informational goodies. Having it on top of the bag like this, it's much closer to your eyes than if it were just lying on the floor (Figure 2-6).

Figure 2-6

EPIDERMASHEET

Finally, while writing on your skin doesn't really seem like a making "cheatsheet," per se, it is essentially the same thing. (Also, we couldn't really think of anywhere else better in this book to mention this technique.) The principle is pretty simple, and doesn't need much explanation. You just write a couple of key things somewhere on your skin if you don't want to fool around with the dangers of pulling out a real cheatsheet in class. But there are some things to bear in mind:

1. Pencil doesn't work. Felt tip pens are best. Ball points work pretty well too.

2. Never write on the back of your hand. It's just stupid, for obvious reasons. (For the really dense ones out there, it's because people can see it, namely the teacher.)

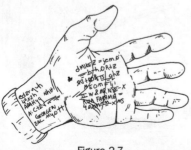

Figure 2-7

3. Your off-hand palm is a very good place to write stuff (Figure 2-7). Sweaty palms are your only enemy.

4. The inside of your wrist is an excellent spot. It's smooth, less hairy (hope-

fully), and shielded from the teacher's eyes not only by the other side of your arm, of course, but by the long sleeves of your shirt, as discussed in Chapter 5.

5. Your legs (if not too hairy) can also be good spot, as discussed in Chapter 5 as well.

6. If a teacher or tattle-tale seems threatening, all you have to do to get rid of skin writing is apply a little saliva, rub away, and, to quote the old Didi-Seven infomercial, "Watch it magically disappear!"

OOPS! WE ALMOST FORGOT . . .

Those rare open-notes/open-book tests. The mentality for these types of tests should be pretty easy to figure out by this point: Exploit them for everything they're worth.

☑ If it's only an open notes test, bring everything you can get your hands on, including old tests. Remember, they're legal. And if necessary, bring in CliffNotes as well, bright yellow covers ripped off though, of course, as discussed in Chapter 10.

☑ If it's only an open book test, fill out a couple of sheets of paper with all the stuff from the notes, shrink them down on the photocopy machine, and then tape them inside the book on pages that don't pertain to the test material (Figure 2-8). Coverless CliffNotes can also be smuggled in through the middle of a large enough book.

Figure 2-8

Chapter 3

State
Dependence Theory

In the last chapter, we reminded you that this is a book of cheating tactics and not learning efficiency methods. Like any good politician, though, we're going to have to go right back on our word, because this, the very next chapter, has absolutely nothing to do with cheating. In fact, you could even say it deals exclusively with a learning efficiency method. So why are we including it? Because we're going to discuss some dimensions of this method that you could *never* find in one of those hunky-dory *How to Get Straight A's (and a Date for the Prom, too!)* books that your mom has been stuffing in your stocking for the last three years, much to your chagrin.

The State Dependence Theory is a pretty straight-forward idea from psychology, so we'll keep our discussion of it short and concise. (Having, of course, already spent an entire paragraph above rambling on about pretty much nothing.) The State Dependence Theory postulates that the mind associates certain cognitive processes with certain conditions and environments. What? Basically this just means that if you learn something in a certain place or state of mind, your chances of recalling that information later are better if you can return to that certain place and/or state of mind.

In other words, if your brain is used to dealing with mathematics at ten o'clock in the morning every day while you sit in the third seat from the left in the back row of Room 101, then you better damn well sit in the third seat from the left in the back row of that ten o'clock class when you're taking the test! (Of course, there are other, more important seating considerations, as discussed in Chapter 6, but still keep all this in mind.) In fact, there are even State Dependence fanatics who go so far as to say that not only should you sit in the same seat every day, but you should also use the same pencil and even wear the same outfit every day so that your mind is completely used to that exact environment when dealing with the given subject. Following these suggestions would actually make you the ideal cheater, because then you could wear your Cheating Uniform (see Chapter 5) every day and the teacher wouldn't be suspicious on test day. (Of course, the entire student body would be suspicious about you in general, and your social life would probably take a nosedive, so. . .)

Alright, let's get to the part they can't talk about in books like *Wow, Mom! I Never Knew Learning Could Be So Much FUN!* or *Jimmy's Not Really the Milkman's Kid: How Your Screw-up Kid Can Learn More Effectively.* Yes, the state of mind thing. We obviously can't advocate the use of substances, *but if you can get your hands on some Ritalin. . .* No. Just kidding. Seriously, though, the State Dependence deal works the same for the environment around your brain as the environment *in* your brain. In other words, if you drink a cup of coffee every day before your biology class, then your brain is used to being under the influence of caffeine when learning biology. Therefore, make sure you drink coffee on test day as well. (Duh!)

And believe it or not, those of you who study or go to class every day feeling a little, uh, "light-headed," we'll carefully say, should take the test in that same state of mind. The State Dependence proponents really say this. But hey, even if this doesn't work, at least you'll have an excuse for bombing that one test. (Though that excuse obviously wouldn't cut it with your parents, only with yourself.)

Finally, speaking of Ritalin, IT WORKS. Enough said. Take it when you are both studying *and* taking the test the next day—that is, of course, only if you have a prescription. Eh hem.

Chapter 4

The Dreaded Monster: Test Day

It is here. You can no longer escape it. You can no longer procrastinate. And you can no longer hide from its loathsome face... those twisted, snarled, pus-oozing fangs... those bleary, bloody, sallow yellow eyes... that blistered, bloated, and warted slithering tongue... Oh God, it's terrible... it's horrid... it's... it's... *the Test.* The test that you're not nearly ready for, to be more specific. Yes, that very same test that only last night seemed so far away, so distant, so not very imposing. But now it's here. It's really here.

The sun is shining brightly. Your brain doesn't feel like it's going to be alive anytime before lunch. Your oft forgotten hatred of "morning people" is renewed as you gaze at the freaks *jogging* in the freezing morning air on your way to school. And worst of all. . . the material is impossible. You barely know any of it.

No, wait. The true worst of all is that it's not even that hard, really. No, it's not that hard at all, actually. You just ran out of time to learn it. "Oh if I'd only stayed on top of things this semester!" you scold yourself. "If I had just gone to every class, paid attention, and done the damn ten minutes of homework every night, I wouldn't have to study or even cheat at all! I'd get straight A's!" You go through this same fruitless ritual every time, don't you? Yes, you do. We all do.

We all invariably come to this point countless times during our academic career, but kicking ourselves isn't going to get us more points on the test— only cheating is. That's right, the test is only a short while away, so it's time to stop torturing yourself with "What could have been." Such nonsense is completely useless and irrelevant at this point. You must turn your thoughts now to "What can I do to keep from failing this freakin' thing?"

Well, basically, there are two paths you can take. No, not To Cheat or Not To Cheat. When you're just about completely screwed an hour to go before the test, cheating is unavoidable. The true question is. . .

TO GO OR NOT TO GO

Yes, that is the question. Whether 'tis nobler in the mind to suffer the slings and arrows of outrageous test problems, or to take arms against a sea of troubles, and by staying home, end them. . . and by a sleep to say we end the heartache. To sleep, perchance to dream—aye, there's the rub, for in that sleep what dreams may come of having to take the test the very next day anyway? Okay, we know, enough. For those of you who didn't have a barfbag handy, sorry about that. Couldn't resist.

What we're talking about here is the frequent dilemma on test day of whether to go to school and just get the test over with or to stay home, claim sickness, and take it some time in the near future.

OPTION 1: GETTING IT OVER WITH

As with any option, this one has pros and cons.

Pros

Exactly that—getting it over with and nipping your anxiety in the bud. More importantly, though, taking the test on test day enables you to cheat off the many other students who are also taking it then. Refer to the following couple of chapters, which are devoted to what to do if you opt to take the test at its slated date.

Cons

The cons of going are dependent on what you're giving up by staying home, as discussed in the section below. Basically, there are a lot of variables that might keep you from being able to cheat in class. It's a big gamble. The teacher might spontaneously decide that you should sit in the front row, or perhaps even that she, the teacher, is going to sit near you for some odd reason. Also, the kid you were going to cheat off of might not show up. Or, worst case scenario, the test might just be flat out impossible and all the in-class cheating in the world isn't going to help you so much as even pass.

OPTION 2: GETTING "SICK"

Alright, now we're talking. Skipping a test is always a good move if done properly and, more importantly, in moderation. If your attendance record is perfect (yeah right) except for four days which "just happen" to coincide with the four test dates, the teacher is probably going to catch on. Remember, teachers aren't dumb people, they're just people too lazy to get real, year-round jobs. Skip tests in moderation. They usually get harder as the year goes on, so you probably want to save this maneuver for tests *after* the first test (also, the farther into the semester, the more you're usually behind, right?). Right.

Pros
One, you get to stay home and either sleep for twelve hours (college) or watch a lot of really good junk TV

(if you're in high school): *The Price Is Right*, *Springer*, a *Gilligan* rerun here, a random USA Network game show there, a made-for-TV movie from the late seventies, *Happy Painting with Bob Ross*, and maybe a soap or two. Plus, all that good junk food.

Two, you can find out what's on the test! Just call someone you know and find out the questions. Even if the teacher changes the problems, you'll have a good idea about what type of stuff you'll need to know (or at least write on your cheatsheet). And teachers do change the problems sometimes, so make sure you don't just waltz in and scribble down yesterday's answers to today's new and slightly altered questions; check out the horror story about this in Chapter 13, "So Close! But No Cigar." (Also, there's a lesson to be learned from Bart Simpson in the episode where he stays home, gets the answers from Milhouse, then waltzes into class the next day and cockily jots down the answers—only to find out later that Milhouse's answers were all wrong. They both fail. Advice: ask your friend who took it about the *questions*, not the "answers.")

Third—and this is a big one—you will often get to take the makeup test somewhere like an empty room or out in the hallway ALONE. That's right—solo, unsupervised, and unstoppable. This, of course, means you cheat like mad, blatantly pulling out your cheatsheets, notes, and even textbooks if you can. Don't get carried away, though. You never know when the teacher might just "pop in" on you. It's best to make one gigantic, info-packed cheatsheet on a full

Figure 4-1

sheet of paper, and then just place it right under the test you are taking (Figure 4-1). This way, to refer to it, all you have to do is peel back your test, as opposed to constantly digging through your pockets or constantly shifting things around.

As far as the textbook goes, be careful. If you bring it in, just leave it on the floor and leaf through it with your feet (Figure 4-2). It's usually better, though, to just leave it in the bathroom like you would

for a normal test (see Chapter 7).

If you wind up taking the test in the teacher's office alone, lock the door (unless they specifically tell you not to) so that you'll be able to know when

Figure 4-2

someone's coming and you can stash your stuff. If you're really lucky, there will be a corrected copy of the test lying around, but if there's not, DO NOT search through the office. (No matter how much of a slob they are, the teacher will probably notice, and not take too kindly to it either.) If the teacher asks why you locked the door when they come back, say you thought you were supposed to lock it, that you thought you weren't supposed to be disturbed by anyone. The teacher might even think you didn't want students dropping in and possibly helping you. (Yeah right!)

Fourth, in the best-case scenario (realistically), the teacher will hand back the tests before you take yours. Then, obviously, you just learn that stuff or even bring it to the empty room that you take the makeup in. Again, avoid just memorizing answers and copying them down onto the makeup carelessly, and never, NEVER GIVE YOURSELF 100 ON AN EXAM. Always get at least two answers wrong on purpose. This is a golden rule of cheating. No teacher in the world is dumb enough not to put two and two together when a slapdick like you gets 100 on a makeup test when the originals have already been handed back to your buddies.

Fifth, in the best-case scenario (unrealistically), if the teacher gives you the makeup test to either take home or stick in his mailbox whenever you finish it, you can take it to someone—a friend or a professional—who can do it for you and give you that 98 you've always dreamed of.

EXCUSES EXCUSES EXCUSES

Well, well, well. Decided to play a little hooky, did we? And what do you have to say for yourself, young man?

Don't panic. If you have half a clue, killing the teacher's suspicions with a good lie—oops, we meant "excuse"—is easier than stealing candy from a Seven-Eleven. . . er, uh, we mean, a "baby." The key, though, is not just *what* you tell them, but *when* and *how* you tell them. In this regard, high school and college are two different worlds altogether.

HIGH SCHOOL

In high school, all that matters is being excused by your mom. It wouldn't matter if you wound up running a marathon that day, so long as the school got a phone call that morning from your parent (or someone impersonating your parent) verifying that you are in fact "gravely ill." How you go about this is up to you. All parents are different, and we're not going to waste time telling you how to work your parents. Surely you've figured out some approach by now. If you haven't, then it's a wonder that you even got this book past them.

COLLEGE

In college, things get a bit more complicated. Think about it. Your parents only get "sick" excuses and the like from you and maybe a couple of other siblings at the most. College professors, on the other hand, deal with literally hundreds of excuses from all sorts of kids every semester, week in and week out, particularly around exam and term paper deadline time. In one brief, twelve-week semester, a professor is liable to find himself teaching a class that is home to every disease and family tragedy known to the modern world. Come to think of it, can you name another profession where someone has to sort through so many pathetic b.s. excuses? (Well, at least from people who aren't trying to avoid going to jail?) As such, it takes considerably more skill to get out of a test with a seasoned college professor than it does to get out of mowing the lawn at home. Here are some approaches if. . .

You Talk to the Professor Before the Test

Depending on your relationship with the professor and/or their policies, you might want to tell them in advance that you are going to miss the test. When you just flat out don't show up for a test, the professor is likely to think you just got too hammered the night before and slept through it. A simple phone call to the professor the morning of the test almost always makes your story more believable. So, if you can, follow the steps and do it. (And if you can't it's no biggie, as you'll see in the next section).

STEP 1: GET UP! Wake up at around seven or eight in the morning. (Don't worry, you'll only have to be awake for two minutes). Ideally, you want to get the teacher's answering machine or voice mail. That way, the teacher knows that you were actually awake that morning but not necessarily hung over, and you can just deliver your excuse without any cross-examination. Also, you'll probably be so tired at this ungodly hour that you really will sound ill.

STEP 2: LEAVE THE MESSAGE. Push through those beer-cans-converted-into-ashtrays on your night table to grab the phone, then call the teacher up and leave a message saying you're "really sick and don't think I'll be able to make it to the test. I'm really sorry for the inconvenience. I'll call or meet with you tomorrow to see when I can take it if I'm feeling better." That's it. Keep it short and sweet. Don't offer any more information than you have to. If the teacher wants to know exactly what was wrong with you, he can ask you later. The only other thing you might want to add at this point, though, is that you "have to go to the doctor"; then, later if you need to, you can say your appointment conflicted with the original test time.

STEP 2A: TELLING HIM LIVE. If the teacher is there after all and answers the phone, just tell him the same thing. If he says he needs proof, tell him you are scheduled to go the infirmary later, and that you'll bring the pink slip/receipt. If he's still not satisfied (the prick) and says that he needs a phone call from the doctor, tell him your appointment is not until much later and that'll you get the doctor to call, which you will.

Speaking of which, while you're awake, also call the school infirmary and make an appointment for later.

STEP 3: ZZZ'S. Go back to sleep. Ahhh, yes. Sleeeeeeep. Nothin' like it. Snore away. Dream away. Drool away. You might as well enjoy some good sleep for the all the work you're going to have do later in the afternoon for this scam. (Actually, there's not much work to be done at all; but, as you certainly know by now, in college a good chance to sleep in should never be passed up.)

STEP 4: GO TO INFIRMARY. When you finally get up, lug your lazy ass over to the school infirmary. Don't worry about working yourself up to seem sick, like in *E.T.* when the kid sticks his head under hot lamps to fabricate a fever.

STEP 5: GETTING DOC TO CALL PROF. In the rare event that the teacher wants a phone call from the doctor, just wait out your appointment, go in there, and tell the doctor the magic excuse—the Golden Lie of Getting Out of Things: *Diarrhea*. That's right. The runs, Hershey squirts, whatever you want to call 'em. Suck up your pride and just flat out tell the doctor, "I've been having really bad diarrhea all last night and this morning and I couldn't make a test today. In fact, I wouldn't have even made it over here today either except that my professor wanted you to verify that I'm sick, so could you please call him for me?" Of course he can! What do think he's going to do, ask for proof? For samples? Like, "Well, son, I don't know. You better drop yer' drawers and lemme get a whiff o' that." Hell no he won't! He'll probably want you out of his office ASAP. Diarrhea: the Golden Excuse. Don't forget it. And don't try to get creative and think of something else. Nothing is better.

STEP 5A: PICK YOUR OWN DISEASE. If the professor doesn't need a phone call from the doctor, then you don't even have to *see* the doctor. But wait a minute—don't break out the smoking apparatus just yet. You still need to go to the infirmary. But all you have to do (at most schools, anyway) is walk in and say you just need to go to the pharmacy. The receptionist should give you the standard medical record printout slip with all the diseases listed and a box for the total charge on it. Then you just walk into the pharmacy room, charge some stuff (toothbrush, vitamins, whatever), check out, and leave. Now you have a pink slip from the infirmary.

But what about my disease, you ask? Just find some carbon paper somewhere (credit card slips are good), stick it between the pink slip and another piece of paper (Figure 4-3), and just check off the ailment of your choice! Typhoid, syphilis, ebola—you name it, you got it! Hallelujah!

Seriously, though, stick to the simpler ones, like a fever, stomach flu, or pharyngitis (the common cold).

Figure 4-3

STEP 6: BRING THE EVIDENCE. Meet with your professor, either after the next class or sooner. Have the slip folded up in your hand, ready to present—but don't show it to him unless he asks for it. A lot of times if they just see pink paper in your hand they've seen enough. (This mentality can lead to trouble, though, if one time you decide to just bring an old slip and have it in your hand, banking on the teacher not checking it out— and then he does.)

Set up a time to take the makeup. Try to get it for during the next class, so that you'll be unsupervised. Remember, this person doesn't know if you work forty hours a week or if you're a trust fund kid, so feel free to shoot down any of their suggestions with "I can't. I have to work then." Or, "I can't. I have class then."

They might confront you first, though, with something like "Okay, what's your schedule?" To prepare for this question, check the professor's office hours on the syllabus, and say you have class during those times. That way, you avoid taking the test in their office with them sitting there hovering over you.

STEP 7: GO, DAMN IT! Show up for the makeup time you have scheduled and get it over with. A major trap students often fall into is once they've missed the initial test time, it gets easier and easier to miss the makeup times. The next thing you know, you're either looking down the barrel of an F or you're taking the damn thing on Christmas Eve.

You Don't Talk To the Professor Until After You've Missed the Test. . .

You bum. Couldn't even get up for the thirty seconds required to leave a message on your professor's answering machine, eh? Well, there's nothing wrong with that. In fact, more often than not, you're going to wind up giving your teachers excuses *after* the fact than before it. Why? Because a lot of times you won't even decide to get "sick" until moments before the test. You'll be sitting there "studying" at the last minute—i.e., cramming all the things you can onto your cheatsheet and running around trying to find people who took the test in the morning section—and as the clock ticks faster and faster to the dreaded hour, you'll come to the conclusion that the only way you can keep from failing this thing is by skipping it and taking it later. So you say "screw it," pack up your stuff, tell your buddy to remember what's on the test, and go home, figuring you'll worry about it later. Either that, or you just flat out slept through class.

Whatever the case, now it's later, and it's time to figure out what you're gonna do. No problem. Just do step 5a above, then call the teacher either while the test is still going on, or after five o'clock so you know he won't be there. Leave a message saying you were sick, and then go up to him right before the next class period and talk to him in person to schedule a makeup time.

Drastic Measures

If the professor is less than cool about missing tests because of "illnesses," then you're going to have to dig a little deeper into the moral bag. Yes, you're going to have tell a big lie, not a just a little one like "I had the runs, sir." You're going to have to call him the day after the test and explain that you couldn't make it because of one of the following:

A. *Funeral.* You had to fly home yesterday on short notice because of a sudden death in the family. For karma purposes, make up a relative you don't really have, like a "grand uncle" or something. This excuse is a rough one, we know, so please use it sparingly, only in the most utterly desperate situations—and not more than once per semester, for God's sake (literally).

B. *Family crisis*. You had to go home because the family's in shambles after your parents' sudden decision to get a divorce, or after your sister got in that awful accident, or now that your brother's going to jail and/or into rehab, or now that your mother is drinking again, etc. No professor is going to want to pry any further into such sticky subjects. Plus, how well can the professor expect someone to concentrate under such circumstances? Chalk up the sympathy points. If you use something along these sketchy lines, you should skip the next class too, because you probably wouldn't fly all the way home for just one day, now, would you?

You Know You're Going To Miss the Test Far in Advance

This is mainly for when you have a test on a Friday but don't want it to get in the way of the big weekend you've got lined up. Let's say you have a wedding to go to, a big concert out of town you've been waiting for, or just a monstrous Thursday night party coming up. Well, sorry to break it to you, but you're going to have to dance along that gray and spotty moral line and use one of the above two methods, A or B.

The only difference is that you do so a couple of days before the test, as opposed to a couple of days after. For a Friday test, tell the professor after class on Wednesday that you're leaving immediately for the funeral or wedding or whatever. Ideally, the teacher would like it best if you told them about such pre-engagements at the beginning of the semester. But if you do that, you run the risk of the teacher scheduling you to take the test *before* you leave, and then you're worse off than if you didn't tell them anything at all.

You Barely Remember Where the Classroom Is

In other words, you've missed not just a day or two, but more like a month or two. If the professor hasn't tracked you down or automatically dropped you from the class yet, there's only one thing to do. Drag your sorry butt into his office and lay on him (or her) one heavy, ton-of bricks word: *Rehab.* That's right. Rehab. And don't even say what kind unless they specifically ask, which they most likely won't. Again, no professor is going to want to pry into your personal life and possibly push a wrong button, so just keep 'em guessing. They'll wonder: Alcohol? Cocaine? An eating disorder? Prescription pills? Depression? Heroin? Pedophilia? *My God, what the hell is wrong with this poor kid?*

Chapter 5

The Cheater's Uniform

Okay, so you're taking the plunge after all (*suck-errr...*). No, just kidding. Despite the almost guaranteed successes of staying home and taking the makeup, there is a lot to be said for going on the actual test day and getting it over with. Besides, you *have* to go to some tests. Unless you're on permanent life-support, no teacher is going to buy it if you miss every test. So, here we go: What do you need to wear? Obviously, we know that at this point in your life, social status is probably more important than a couple of points on a test, so we don't expect anyone to actually don the full getup like the goofball shown in Figure 5-1. We just wanted to wrap all your options into one "nifty" little package.

1: Hat
Preferably long-billed (but not so much as to look ridiculous), and curved as well. This essential device

Figure 5-1

is used primarily to shield the eyes as they freely wander from test to test, neighbor to neighbor. Works best when worn really low, redneck-style. Also, when removed and placed on the desk (often mandatorily), the hat can also be a good, albeit risky, source of crib notes. Be aware, though, that it is much wiser to have a paper cheatsheet sitting *inside* the hat, as opposed to inscribing notes in the inside of the bill. (Cheatsheets can be eaten, hats cannot.) Besides, why ruin a good hat or run the risk of having ink run down a sweaty forehead later on? Also, make sure you wear the hat in class a few times before the test date so the teacher is somewhat accustomed to seeing you in it.

2: Eyeglasses
Even if you have 20/20 vision, try to wear some kind of eyeglasses. They work to cloud and obscure the path of your wandering eyes from the teacher or TA, who is always watching, that's right, *YOU*. Remember to be seen in them in class a couple times before. If you're one of those weirdoes who wears tinted glasses all the time, perfect.

3: Beard or Facial Hair
It helps to have a beard or some sort of facial hair, if possible. (Please, though—males only.) This further obscures your eyes from the eyes of those who wouldn't take kindly to your cheatin' ways. With the lowered hat, thick glasses, and beard, your cheating

head will appear as just a cluttered, blurry mess. It may not look that great, but who cares? These are sorely needed grade points we're talking about here.

4: Long Sleeve Pocket T-shirt

The long sleeves are necessary to cover wrists and forearms which have notes, equations, or other helpful hints written all over them. The chest pocket can house a cheatsheet or two. Cheatsheets can also be lodged under the elastic wrist-cuffs for easy access. Ink usually runs, though, so pick your shirt accordingly. For all clothing, choose dull colors. Don't draw any unnecessary attention to yourself by wearing some loud, *Brady Bunch*–looking piece of apparel.

OPTIONAL: Though hot, it can be very useful to wear a pullover jacket or hooded sweatshirt with one of those large front pockets on the belly. This pocket can hold a lot of notes and can easily be accessed by either hand.

5: Calculator Watch

Self-explanatory. And preferably not one from a gumball machine.

6: Belt

The important thing here is to choose a belt with a readily accessible buckle large enough to stuff cheatsheets in. (Next time you watch *Dazed & Confused*, take note of Randall "Pink" Floyd's bud-stashing buckle.)

7: *Lengthy shorts or skirt*

Weather permitting, of course. This provides cover for the thighs, an excellent place to write notes. One, you can easily hold your forehead and look down at them as if you're racking your brain over the given problem. Two, and best of all, in these ultrasensitive times no teacher will have to the gall to ask to inspect anywhere near the ol' genitalia and run the risk of the big Sexual Harassment Suit.

8: *Jeans*

If either Jack Frost or your school's dress code mandates that you cover the legs, go with an old beat-up pair of jeans with as many holes as *reasonably* possible (i.e., leave the 1987 commemorative Def Leppard pair at home). This way, you can write answers directly on your legs and then shift the jeans in mid-test so that the holes line up with the notes and reveal them. Writing on the jeans themselves, where the teacher could easily see your handiwork as you sashay out of class, is asking for it. Don't do it.

If your school dress code mandates that your jeans be holeless or that you not wear jeans at all, but khakis or a uniform instead, then there's not much else we can tell you, other than that your school is pretty lame.

9: *Tight, Calf-length Socks*

Wear these scrunched down to your desire. (We don't expect *any* one to wear knee-length socks, though they would be best.) Yet another fine stashing place for cheat-sheets, accessed with a sly scratch of the lower leg.

10: High-topped Shoes

Basketball shoes or hiking boots fit the bill here. Once again, a good stashing place. Don't fool around with writing on them, though, as they are not cover-up-able, are expensive, and are about as close to your eyes as they are to the teacher's eyes. Take a lesson from the great Mike Seaver of *Growing Pains*, who got caught when kicking his feet up onto a desk in relaxation. (And, on that note: Never celebrate prematurely! In fact, try not to do *anything* prematurely.)

ADDITIONAL AIDS WORTHY OF CELEBRATION, BUT JUST TOO DANGEROUS TO ACTUALLY USE

The immortal cheating icon, Chevy Chase's Emmit Fitzhume in *Spies Like Us*, was the true master. The following should be remembered and smiled upon, but seldom used:

The fake eye patch with answers inscribed within it (Figure 5-2). If you actually wear an eye patch, then you may want to go for it. Wait—come to think of it, if you actually wear one, that eye probably can't read it as you pull it out, right? Sorry. Never mind.

Figure 5-2

The fake arm cast and sling, chock-filled with notes (Figure 5-3). There's at least one plus to having a broken arm besides all the attention and excuses to get out of doing chores. So if you actually do have on a cast,

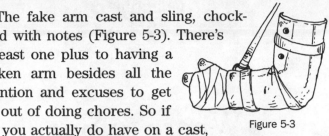

Figure 5-3

use it. But if you don't have a broken arm, don't bother with a fake cast. What the hell are you going to do, keep wearing it for six weeks?

Finally, the laminated, foldable strip of notes that looks like a stick of chewing gum (Figure 5-4). Ah, a moment of silence for the great Fitzhume.

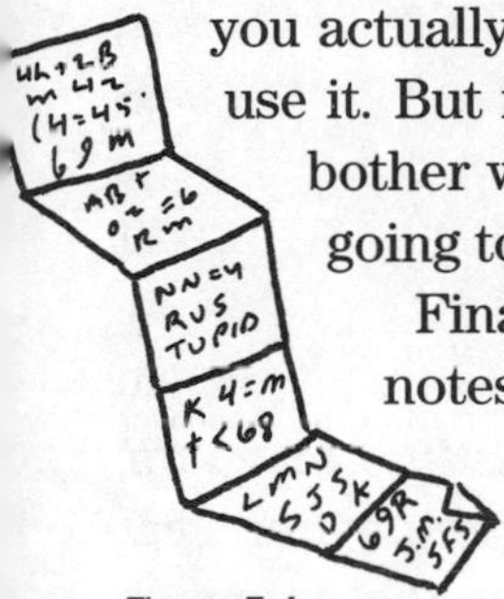

Figure 5-4

Chapter 6

Where to Sit

Picking your seat may a favorite pastime of yours, but when it comes to actually *choosing* your seat before the test starts (ha. . . ha), realize that this may very well be the most important strategic decision of your life. Okay, well, maybe just your day. Any*wayz*, be sure to run each of the following through your frayed mind whenever entering the dreaded classroom on test day.

COPYING OFF SOMEONE

Never be the first one to arrive, even if you think you're positive about where the person you want to copy off of will sit. If you're the first one to arrive and you stand there goofily and fidget around while everyone who comes in after you takes their seats, people might get suspicious. Suspicion leads to paranoia, and the next thing you know, your ticket to an A has boxed himself in the corner behind three other people. The A-Man will also be *very* suspicious if he walks in to find you've suddenly had a "change of heart," or suddenly "just happen" to be sitting in the front row next to where he always sits, when all year long you've darted straight to the back row and spent most of your class time either catching up on sleep or playing Gameboy with the volume down.

Fiddle out in the hall "studying" until you see your target(s) coming. Then, follow into the classroom behind them. Do not make any eye contact with them whatsoever at any point.

For regular *Welcome Back Kotter* or *Head of the Class*–like classrooms (Figure 6-1), it is best to sit directly next to the target, on *the opposite side of their writing hand*. The writing hand's arm obstructs the beeline your eyes will invariably want to make to the kid's test at some point. Sit to the left of a rightie or the right of a leftie, and his desk will be wide open to you.

For lecture rooms (Figure 6-2), it is best to sit one row behind your target, and one seat over, according to the target's writing arm, as discussed above. This diagonal scooping action is perhaps the finest there is, for you can more clearly read *down* onto his paper without the putz realizing it, he concentrating instead on shielding his magic sheet from his neighbors to the right and left.

NOTE: There is a major exception to these rules, however, which arises when the person to be cheated off of is collaborating with you. To best receive the answers from this friend, social climber, or blackmail victim of yours—whatever the case may be—sit directly behind them, and try to have them sit directly in between you and the teacher's line of vision. This way the person can hold his test up in front of his face as if to read it in better light or something, and it can be angled just slightly enough to his right or left so that you can freely read and copy it. Obviousness can often be a great tactic in any underhanded scheme. Remember, though: Be careful with your eyes if the test is not being held up directly in between you and the teacher's head. The ol' lowered bill and/or foggy glasses are essential in this case.

SELF-RELIANCE

Many of us prefer not to put our fate in the hands of others who, no matter how studious they are ordinarily, may have had some kind of disastrous night before the test or have just recently made a spontaneous decision to "walk on the wild side" and blew off studying all week. Thus, we rely on ourselves, and when the knowledge ain't lodged in the noggin, it's sure to be lodged somewhere on our person. So it's time to head straight on to the good ol' back row, baby! This should be no problem, since most of us have already spent the majority of our classes seated towards the back. Why? Who knows. Many do it for its most obvious function: to be as far as possible from the teacher and his painful lessons and question-asking, and to have as many students in between you and him as possible, so as to more effectively goof off, sleep, or play video games. Some do it out of the understandable paranoia of being stared at, fantasized over, or made fun of (like those situated in front of others usually get or at least *feel* like they're getting). And some, rather pathetically, do it merely because it's often considered "cool."

As opposed to the copying-people method, get to class as early as possible, even an hour before if you can (and feel like it). There are two good reasons to do this. First, this allows you to get the best seat in the house, as you're about to see.

For Regular Classrooms
Choose the seat in the very last row in the corner opposite the door. This seat not only hides you from the teacher best, but also decreases the number of students surrounding you who can see what you're doing and possibly give you away.

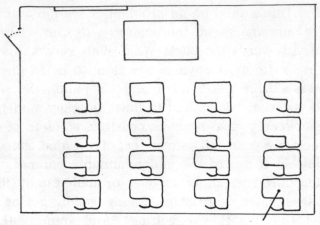

Figure 6-1

For Lecture Rooms

If the seats go all the way to the back wall, you're psyched, because then you can sit in the very middle of the back row and not have to worry about the teacher strolling behind you, looking over your shoulder. And if the room's packed wall-to-wall with students (so the teacher can't get within twenty feet of you) and you're feeling particularly ballsy, you can even spread your actual notebooks and textbooks *open* all over the floor at your feet! Do this only, though, if you know that the people next to you are cool about it. Remind them that they can use the notes too. For other lecture rooms, pretty much any seat in the back will usually do—though sometimes

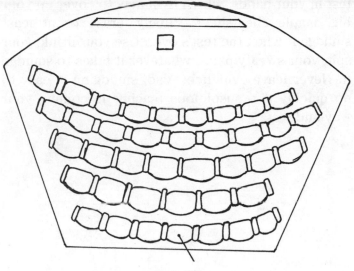

Figure 6-2

it's better to be buried somewhere in the middle of the room if you know that no one else cares that you're cheating. If everyone's a tight-ass, just head for a back corner.

The second reason for getting to class early is that it allows you to put notes in one of the best and least-known spots to teachers and students alike: the desk. That's right, just bring a pencil or felt-tip pen and copy the key dates, names, equations, or whatnot right down in front of you on your desk. Obviously, dark desks won't do. Be sure to do it quickly and discreetly. More importantly, be sure to cover it up with your notebook until you have the test in your hands, which then acts to cover up your big, maple cheatsheet. Finally, erase or at least smudge it when the test's over. Use your drink, your spit, your sweaty palm, whatever it takes to smudge it. Never leave evidence! Also, smudging is easy to do quickly if a suspicious teacher is coming your way mid-test.

Chapter 7

Prestidigitation

Presta-what? All this word means is "sleight of hand," which is what you'll be doing now that you're fully garbed in your cheating uniform and situated in your proper seating arrangement.

That is, of course, if the following situation sounds familiar: The last couple of students are making their way into the classroom. The teacher is standing there tapping his foot, stack of tests in hand, and staring at these bumbling latecomers as they seem to take forever to find a seat and sit down. They eventually do, and the room falls to a dead silence except for maybe that one cough or sniffle coming from somewhere across the room. "Put your notes away, get a pen ready, and keep your eyes off your neighbor's papers please, *people*," the teacher says, or something along those lines. "Take one, pass the rest, and don't begin until I say." Everyone's getting a test. You're trying to sneak a look at yours to see how hard this momma's going to be, and finally, after a couple ticks of the clock, the teacher says "You may begin." The room exhales, tests are flipped over, and it seems that everyone else somehow begins writing things.

But not you.

You're just sitting there. Looking at this thing. Going, "Oh, God, here we go again. Should've studied more."

Yeah, well, that's a nice thought. But you didn't. Once again, you kept procrastinating. First you told yourself, "Okay, after this TV show's over I'll start studying." But then the promo for the show on after that just simply mesmerized you. So you watched the next show. And the next show. And the next one. Finally, when it came down to choosing between the late-night Get-Rich-Quick infomercial with the Japanese guy on the yacht or an old rerun of *Vega$*, you figured it was time to get up and do something.

So you did. You turned on the video game system. You figured it would be better to just get the craving out of the way before you tackled all that monstrous studying. And so even though you'd already beaten every game you own, you played every single one again, timing yourself now, though, seeing how fast you could beat each one. Your most recent record for beating "Bloodbath III: Psycho Slaughterer's Re-Awakening" was eighteen minutes, and you'd be damned if you were going to start studying before you topped that feat.

Finally, with that out of the way, you ran out of options. So you went to your room to start studying. Yeah, you figured it was about that time.

Problem was, though, when you got to your room and pulled out your books and sat down at your desk, you looked around for a minute and realized that there was just no way you could possibly get anything done until your room was clean.

So even though you hadn't either cleaned your room or done your laundry once all year, you were now exploring the joys of alphabetizing your scattered CDs and color-coding your dirty socks.

And the sad saga continued. . .

And so now here you are once again, staring blankly at a gleaming white stack of photocopies stapled together, and you don't have a clue. You've followed all the steps in this book up to this point, but despite our dim promise that you might actually learn some of the stuff on the way, you didn't. Well guess what:

It's time to break out the cheatsheets and/or rob your "neighbor" of answers.

POINTERS FOR COPYING

☑ As discussed in the previous chapter, you should have situated yourself in the proper copying position.

☑ Lower your hat. Also, if your prime target is seated to your right, rotate your hat about ten degrees to the left. (Vice-versa if the person is on your left.) This creates the illusion that you are looking straight forward at *your* test when in fact your head is turned slightly to lessen the strain on your eyes while checking out your *neighbor's* test (Figure 7-1).

Figure 7-1

☑ Sometimes you can just turn your whole body toward your target as if your manner of handwriting made you sit that way or, if you're big, as if you don't fit in the seat properly (Figure 7-2). This is another one of those things that you need to do in classes prior to the test so that the teacher has seen you like this before.

Figure 7-2

☑ Use a pencil so that you can get up and sharpen it several times during the test. These trips allow you to get a really good shot of the main test you're copying, plus quick glimpses of other tests along the path to the pencil sharpener.

☑ After some students have handed in their tests, go up and ask the teacher some banal question about a problem, and try to get a look at those savory handed-in ones sitting right there.

☑ If you're in cahoots with the person next to you, use primitive, eye-contactless, nonverbal communication. (First, have a signal worked out with them before the test to mean SOS, like a clearing of the throat or three taps of your pencil on the desk.)

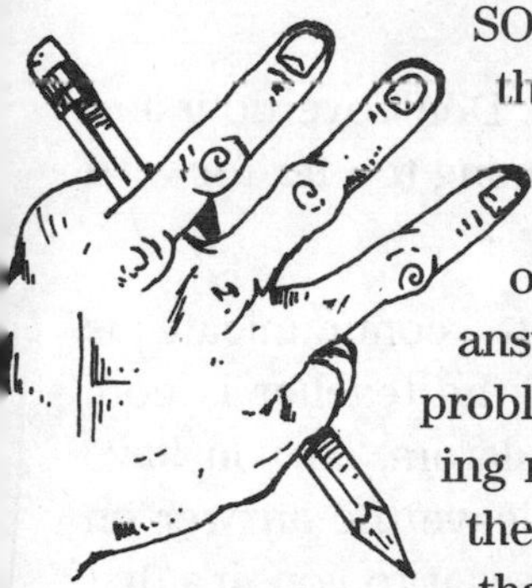

Second, indicate the number of the problem you want the answer to. If it is one of the first five problems, just hold up the corresponding number of fingers (Figure 7-3). If the number of the problem is more than five, write the number of the problem either on your desk or on the top corner of the bottom of the last page (Figures 7-4, 7-5). Your chum should respond in the same manner. *NEVER COMMUNICATE OUT LOUD!!!*

Figure 7-3

☑ If the person in front of you is holding up their test for you to check out, remember to angle your head so that the test is directly between

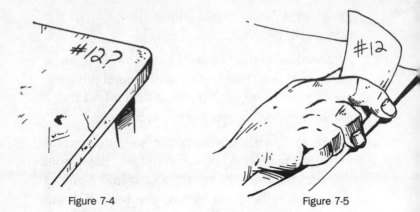

Figure 7-4   Figure 7-5

your eyes and the teacher's. Don't overdo it and fall out of your chair by leaning too far forward or anything.

☑ Another nonverbal way to communicate is through your calculator. If the teacher is cool about people sharing calculators, all you have to do is have your buddy leave the answer on his calculator when he passes it to you. It's that simple, though sometimes it's hard to break out of the habit of pressing the "clear" button after a computation. Even better, if it's one of those super-calculators that can do everything from subtraction to taking the SATs for you, you can communicate actual words to each other.

☑ When you're looking at someone else's paper, it always helps to make it look like you are actu-

ally writing and thus working on
your own test. Just move your
pencil around as if you're
writing, but with the tip
almost (but not quite)
touching the surface
of the paper (Fig-
ure 7-6).

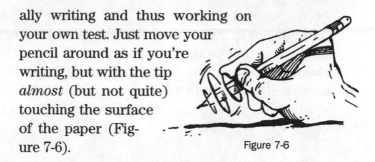

Figure 7-6

☑ As hard as it is to resist, you must try to refrain
from constantly looking up at the teacher to see
if he is watching you copy. That is usually the
first thing that *makes* them think someone is
copying. Seeing as how you just about never
look up at them during regular classes, why the
hell else would you be checking them out during a test unless you're hiding something?

POINTERS FOR USING CHEATSHEETS

This is where the sleight-of-hand thing comes into
play. Pulling out your cheatsheet is a very dangerous
thing. (In fact, of all the things you could possibly pull
out, there's only one thing that could get you into
more trouble, but we won't talk about that here. Then
again, sometimes pulling out for precautionary reasons is a good thing. Okay, never mind. Enough of the
cheap sexual innuendoes.) Most of what you need to
know about accessing your cheatsheet has already

been discussed in Chapter 5, "The Cheater's Uniform." And none of this stuff is really that hard to figure out on your own anyway. Obviously if you have a cheat-sheet stuck in your high-top shoe, you just pretend to scratch right around there and you grab it. Here are some useful tips, though, that weren't included in that chapter.

☑ The best way to pull out your cheatsheet is to not have to pull it out at all. Just have it crumpled up in your non-writing hand when the tests are being passed out. Then when you get one, wedge the cheatsheet in the stapled, upper left hand corner of any page in the middle of the packet (Figure 7-7). To access it, all you have to do is turn to that page, as if you're checking out the problems on that page.

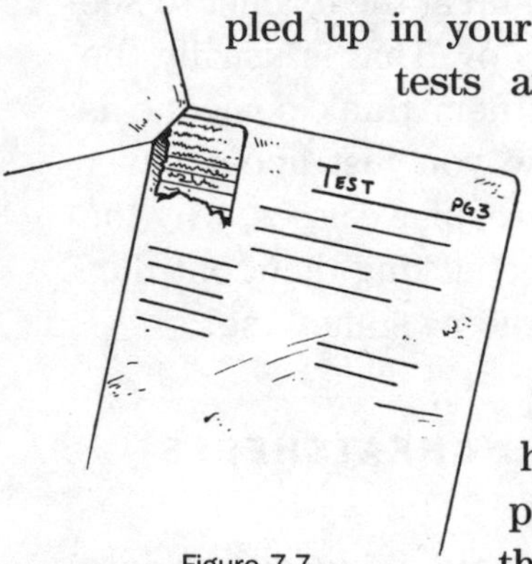

Figure 7-7

☑ Don't forget to crumple up your cheatsheet at the end of the test and either eat it or throw it away somewhere outside of the classroom.

☑ If you forgot to have your cheatsheet ready in your hand when the tests were passed out, and it's still lodged in your outfit somewhere, slyly get it out somehow and do the same thing as above. "Slyly" doesn't mean you reach into your pocket and pull out some suspicious-looking piece of crumpled up paper while all your loose change drops loudly onto the floor (Figure 7-8).

Figure 7-8

Be smart, and very careful. Be subtle when you use such actions as stretching, yawning, coughing, scratching, and the like to cover your moves. Here's a typical three-step process, for example, used to get a cheatsheet from your T-shirt pocket to your desk.

Figure 7-9a

Figure 7-9b

1. Scratch your chest with your right hand, pulling the cheatsheet into your palm while doing so (Figure 7-9a).

2. Place both of your elbows on the desk, rest your chin in your two clenched hands and exhale as if you're taking a momentary breather; during this, the cheatsheet should be transferred to your non-writing hand (Figure 7-9b).

Figure 7-9c

3. Take a big stretch, the cheatsheet now crumpled up in your off-hand. When your hands come back down, grab your pen off the desk with your writing hand, and place your other hand on the test to hold it so you can write. As you do this, let the cheatsheet fall onto the test, which should be opened to a middle page, so that you can then wedge the cheatsheet into the stapled corner (Figure 7-9c).

Figure 7-10

☑ To read stuff written on your palm or wrist, hold your head up with the fingertips of that palm, placing your hand between the teacher's eyes and yours (Figure 7-10).

☑ If you don't have a hat on, read stuff written on your legs by holding your head in the same manner as in Figure 7-10, but with more of a focus on blocking your eyes and tilting your head down.

☑ As with copying, it's always a good idea when you're reading a cheatsheet or something to make it look like you are writing by moving your pencil back and forth but with the tip just millimeters above the paper.

MISCELLANEOUS
ODDS, ENDS, AND TREATS

Your education is not nearly complete, young Jedi of the Dark Side. Last and most certainly not least, here are some extremely important tools of the trade that any budding young deviant such as yourself must be familiar with.

Books in the bathroom

Sorry, master beaters, we're not talking about those books you probably use in the bathroom at home when your mom's out. We're talking about one of the most essential tactics you should employ just about every time you take a test: Leave your stuff in the bathroom. That's right, just leave all those photocopied notes, glossarized textbooks, and purchased study sheets in the bathroom so that you can go in there halfway through the test and look up all the stuff you don't know. Do it *fast*, though. If you spend too much time in there, the teacher's liable to think you fell into the toilet or something, and he might come see if you're alright.

BYOB

That's right, you guessed it: Bring Your Own Bluebook. You know, those standard blue-colored books that they give you for tests with stuff like short-answer questions, essays, etc. Yes, get your paws on a stack of these sometime during the year. This is one of the best cheating methods there is.

You're always allowed to take a couple of bluebooks when they're being handed out so that you won't have to get up and get another one halfway through. Who cares if you've never filled up even half of one these things before? The teacher doesn't know that and won't suspect a thing if he sees that you have two or three on your desk during the test. Because, my friend, you will indeed have two or three—*one of which you brought from home and is completely filled out with as much information as humanly possible.*

All you do is slip it underneath the one(s) the teacher hands you. Then, *no sooner* than fifteen or twenty minutes into the test, you can start shuffling the bluebooks around and referring to the one you brought as if it were simply the first bluebook you had just filled up during the beginning of the test. This is why you must wait twenty minutes, because no one legitimately taking a test could possibly fill up an entire bluebook with meaningful writing in any less time than that.

So what you're basically looking at here if you prepare by filling up *both* sides of *every* page of a bluebook with cheating material is a twenty-page cheatsheet. In fact, come to think of it, the BYOB is the king of all cheatsheets.

But *WATCH OUT*! Occassionally you'll run into the more experienced teacher who has labeled all of the bluebooks with a special stamp. The teacher usually only does this, though, to prevent students from handing in previously filled-out bluebooks when the test questions have been given out prior to the exam. *Don't ever do that.* If the actual test questions are given to the class the day before the test, yes, fill out a bluebook with the answers, of course. But don't hand it in. Spend the exam time copying the information into a fresh bluebook, and making extra sure that they haven't altered any of the questions. Think about it: You have to spend an hour pretending to write stuff anyway.

Frue or Talse?

We mean, true or false. Or do we? Always keep 'em guessing is our motto, and when it comes to True or False questions, you can never spend too much time beforehand perfecting your sloppy, blurry, squiggly-looking *F* that could also be a *T* slash sloppy, blurry, squiggly-looking *T* that could also be an *F* (Figure 7-11). It's hard to get this badgirl right, and even harder to get it to actually work, so use it frugally, on those questions you're *really* in between on. No teacher is going to

Figure 7-11

give a 100 on a True/False test just because he can't tell if that damn symbol is necessarily wrong or not.

But. . . an overworked teacher correcting a mountain of tests might skim over a couple every now and then really fast and not notice that it wasn't the wrong answer, which is all they really look for when *correcting*, now isn't it?

What page?

On that same note of teachers mostly looking for wrong answers, here's a dandy that you can use about once or twice a lifetime. If the test is a large packet of photocopies, say fifteen or more pages thick, and you don't know anything on an entire page that's buried somewhere in the middle, *rip it out and stick it in your pocket.* That's right. Ever-so-gently tear that bad-boy off the staple, make sure there are no remains of it *under* the staple, and smoothly fold it up and stash it when you stand up at the end. Actually, it might be too risky to try this in the classroom, and you probably only want to do it on a makeup test.

It's sweet, though. When your typical teacher or TA is correcting yours, the fiftieth test of the day,[1] they're most likely going to just *add up the wrong answers* and subtract those points from 100, not count all the right ones and add those points up. If they do notice the missing page, they'll probably assume they messed up when coordinating all of those hundreds of sheets into dozens of individual tests.

The A&E Network

No, we're not talking about that channel that has those shows like *Biography of the First Man Who Died in the French-Indian War* that tantalize you so much. We're talking about a tactic that's in the same cheating family tree as good ol' "Frue or Talse." If a test question is multiple choice—but the kind where

---

[1] Make sure your test is one of the last ones to be corrected—i.e., make sure it's at the bottom of the pile. This usually means hand-ing it in last; but if the tests are handed in face-up, stick it under the stack.

you write in the answer as opposed to circling it—
you can make your lowercase *a* look an awful lot like
a lowercase *e* through careful "sloppy" penmanship,
as shown in Figure 7-12). Do this,
though, only in the occasional predica-
ment when you think the answer may
be *a* or *e* but you're not sure.

Figure 7-12

And while we're on the topic of
multiple choice, you can also occassionally circle and cross out and circle again two
answers so that it looks like you've chosen both. How-

1)

2) b

3)

Figure 7-13

ever, you can argue later if necessary
that the right answer is the one you
meant: "See, professor, this one was
crossed out twice, but this one only
once, and then I circled it really hard
again, as you can see, and then *un*circled the other one, and, uh. . . " (Figure 7-13). For a measly two points,
the professor's probably just going to give it to you to
get you out of their face.

Final Friends

In college there are often two or more sections of the
same class, like an eleven o'clock section and a two
o'clock section—same course, same teacher, same
final. If a friend of yours is in another section that is
taking the final before your class does, have him write
down all the questions when they're finished taking it.

Because you get three hours for finals, they're usually the only kind of test that someone would have enough spare time in which to do this.

Whether it's a good friend or not, offer some cash, drinks, or favors for their help. It will take them quite a while to copy all that stuff down, and as you know, *no one* likes being in a test room any longer than they have to be, especially with Christmas or summer break beckoning.

Whoa, Wait a Second

Suppose that right after you hand in your test, you find out some answers for the first page (particularly multiple choice), either by the teacher talking about it or by seeing another student's test on the desk. Try this: Say you think you might've forgotten to put your name on your test and, if the teacher is pretty oblivious, retrieve it and quickly cross out the wrong answer and scribble the right one.

Who is "Someone Who Is Not in My Kitchen"?

We've taken this example from the episode of *Cheers* where Cliff replies to the "Final Jeopardy" question with the above answer (and screw you, Alex, *we're* gonna call it an answer!). Cliff didn't win, of course, but do you get the idea? The key with some teachers is just simply NOT BEING WRONG. Like the SATs, some teachers only subtract points for things that are wrong. So either don't put anything, or put something that is *undeniably not wrong*. For example, Question: "When was the Monroe doctrine indoctrinated?" Possible answers: "Not last year," or "In the 1800s," etc. It's pretty feeble, yeah, but you never know when they're going to start dishing out the partial credit.

"If It Doesn't Fit, You Must Acquit"

From the O. J./Last Ditch Department, one slightly pathetic little stunt you can pull is to write some of your short answers and some por-
tions of essay answers so sloppily that the teacher can't really tell what it says, and thus can't really tell that it's wrong (Figure 7-14). To work, though, it's got to be the right teacher, at the right time (meaning at the peak of their stress cycle and/or apathy cycle), and not overdone.

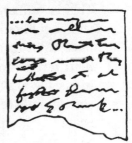

Figure 7-14

Escape Hatch

Finally, one stupid little trick you can do on a test: If you're supposed to write and sign the generic honor code, "I have neither given nor received aid on this assignment," you can "inadvertently" screw it up in your sloppy handwriting so that it says "I have *either* given or received aid on this assignment." It's petty, we know. But it couldn't hurt. Who knows what kind of loophole this could squeeze you through in the event you get caught. You could be like, "Hey, I didn't break the honor code, ma'am. I told you right on the front of the test that I either gave or received aid."

Okay, we admit it—it wouldn't work in a million years. It's just funny, and some people *do* do it.

ONE LAST OPTION:
THE IMMACULATE DECEPTION

This is probably the ultimate cheating scam, and one you should only go for if you're really desperate and/or have a lot of cash. What is it? *Having someone take your test for you.* Yes, we've all thought about it. Some of us have even done it. But should you? Here are some points to consider about different versions of this scam.

SATs

Might as well address the big one on your mind first. The mother of all tests. The mother of all number two pencil manufacturers. The mother of all pains in our respective asses. The S. A. MotherF"ing T's, boy. If you get caught having someone else take the SATs for you or get caught taking them for someone else (probably not too much of an option for scholars of this book), you're absolutely, positively *screwed*. No college will take you, except maybe the local televangelist-owned community part-time junior vo-tech college. WE REALLY DON'T RECOMMEND THIS IDEA.

If you just *have* to do it, though—like if you have to make eligibility for sports (Prop 48) or something—be ultra careful:

☑ Don't hire someone greatly smarter than you. Somebody's going to start snooping around if they see a kid get 1500 on the SATs when that same kid has a C average and made 600 on the PSATs last year. See Chapter 13 for a horror story.

☑ Prepare the person well. Get them a fake ID card with your personal information on it and also give them something else with your name on it, like a video store card. Have them memorize everything about you. Remember, they're going to have to fill out the beginning part that asks for name and address and all that.

☑ Be prepared to shell out some pretty serious bucks, like five hundred or so.

☑ DON'T TELL ANYONE. We repeat: *DO NOT TELL ANYONE!* Yeah, we know if you pull off a great scam like this you're going to want to brag about it left and right, but you just *can't*, dude. A teacher who's "chummy" with the kids (like the "cool coach" who jokes about drinking, etc.), is bound to overhear some jackass running his mouth about it.

If by some freak occurrence you do wind up taking the SATs for somebody else (God help this crumbling nation), here are a couple of tips:

- ☑ Get *paid*. You better be making some serious high school cash on this operation, fool, like five hundred minimum.

- ☑ Run like the wind if you get caught. Screw the guy who's name is filled out in all those little ovals. He was twice the fool to hire YOU.

Other Tests

Have someone else take a regular class test for you ONLY if the class is humongous or if your shill looks exactly like you. We probably don't need to explain to you how risky this is. So we won't. All we have to say is: The person doing it for you better have already taken that class, gotten an A, and have a memory like an elephant; and *you* better be pretty dumb, pretty desperate, and pretty much have an inheritance or something else colossal riding on your grade in that class.

THE WHOLE SHEBANG

Now, if you got the cash, this isn't too bad an idea. It's going to take some *serious* funds, though, to get someone to take an entire course for you. Think about it: Even if you broke it down into hourage and paid a measly five dollars an hour, you're looking at three hours of class time per week for twelve weeks, plus the hundreds of additional hours of homework, studying, and stress. At a real rate that someone would actually go for, you're probably looking at a couple of grand.

This method is pretty foolproof, though, as long as the professor never sees the real you. By far the best time to do it is in summer school. Short and sweet. Taking a class for one month for two grand is a pretty killer summer job, wouldn't you say? Surely you can find someone smart to go for that deal. Just think, you could be sitting pretty by the pool, drinking, soaking up rays, and earning an A at the same time!

But speaking of A's, you better damn well get your money's worth. Tell the guy you'll give him a grand at the beginning and a grand when that big fat A is registered in the school's computer under your name and social security number. Be careful about prorating for lesser grades. If you tell the guy that you're going to knock off two hundred bucks for each letter grade lower than an A, then he just might join you along side the swimming pool and earn $1600 for a measly C, and you wind up getting screwed. Tell him it's a grand for passing, another grand for the A, and a hired-thug, ass-kicking full refund for an F.

Chapter 8

BUSTED!!!: The Code of Damntheygotme

"**O**hhh. . . ffffffffffffffffffffffuuuuuuuuuuuuuuuuuuuuuu-uuuuuuuuuuuuuuuuuuuuuuuuuuuuuuuuuuuuuuuuuuuuuuuuuuu-uuuuuuuuuuuuuuuudge."

You thought we were going to say it, didn't you. Yeah, well, we can't. But you can, and you most certainly will if you ever get caught cheating.

Busted. Snagged. Bagged. Flagged. Apprehended. Nailed. Call it what you will, it all boils down to the same thing: You're in trouble, little buddy. Well, for the moment at least. They say where there is a will, there is way. We say, where there is way, we'll find it. More than one morally bankrupt, utterly depraved, unabashed corner-hopping cheater like yourself has gotten himself out of what initially seemed like a hopeless case of getting caught red-handed. And even if he didn't get out, if he did indeed go down on that black day, he went down alone. For, either way, he—that myth-like legend of many a high school's past glory— intrinsically knew *The Code of Damntheygotme.* Many of you, for that matter, may have always known *The Code* as well. The feel of it just comes naturally with being a born cheater.

But for you newcomers, for you once strapping young scholars who have recently discovered the joys of video games or chronic TV watching or chronic something else and who now wish to join the growing ranks of America's elite underachievers, we will review the basic principles of the awful, unholy process of—Oh God, it hurts to even say it—Getting Caught. Now, the question is, were you. . .

. . . LOOKING AT YOUR "NEIGHBOR'S" PAPER?

The crossfire triangulation will probably go like this: Straining over to see the test you are copying off of, your eyes are almost slipping out of their sockets, intermittently darting over to see if the teacher is looking, and then finally going back to your test so you can write down your newfound knowledge. This process goes on smoothly for a while, to the point that a devilish smirk is beginning to form on your face. . . until suddenly, one of those times when your eyes dart over to check the teacher's—NO!—they lock up with his eyes like a deer in front of a Mack truck's headlights.

Busted. The teacher saw you sneaking peeks. As master Shakespearean thespian Keanu Reeves put it so eloquently in *Speed*, "What do you do?. . . *What* do you do?"

What you do is start changing the answers you copied to wrong ones—as many as you *gracefully* can before the teacher makes his way over to you. This is your only hope. No time for erasing here, just start crossing out copied things and writing new, inane ones. The teacher might have seen your eyes pointed over there, but the only real, hard proof he has that could really be used to punish you (i.e., that he could show to the higher-ups) is your test having the same answers as the one you were looking at.

The key is to remain calm. From the moment your eyes lock up with the teacher's until the time he walks over, just casually keep your lid down (your hat, that is), and start smoothly changing some answers. If nothing else, the teacher's ultimate case will prove inconclusive. Remember O. J.: His freakin' DNA *matched* that of the "killer's," and he still got off! Certainly *you* can beat a measly little *cheating* rap if your answers don't even match up with the right ones.

. . . FULL-ON COPYING?

If you're busted *after* the tests are handed in and corrected—in other words, if the teacher merely finds that you and someone else have conspicuously similar test results—just plead coincidence. The authorities can't *really* prove who copied whom, as long as neither one of you squeals and you say you used the same study sheet. Of course, if you copied off the school brain with a 4.0 GPA., you're not sitting so pretty anymore.

The key here is to take the offensive. Act insulted and unfairly biased against, either because of discrimination (if you're not white) or reverse discrimination (if you're white). These terrifyingly litigious times allow for a lot more weaseling out of things than previous eras. Exploit it. Tell the teacher that your dad's a lawyer and he'll raise hell if the teacher continues with these gross accusations and slanderous defamations, and that you're prepared to go all the way with this matter. That should make them reevaluate just how much they care about this little incident (and perhaps make them consider just assigning seats in the future).

NOTE: Those of you reading this who are now having a little ethical heartburn, we understand. Such Johnnie Cochran–like exploitation and general spinelessness as is being espoused in this section is hard to stomach and to seriously consider for premeditated use. All we can say, though, is when the you-know-what hits the fan and in a flash you're facing the possibility of your whole academic career going down the tubes, you'll be amazed at how quickly your morals will "adapt." Counting on this adjustment, we're here simply to give you advice for such dreadful moments, may they never come. After all, if you feel remorse over telling a lie, you can always confess afterward, to the teacher or your clergyman or both. Whatever. It's all up to you, so don't ever blame this book—or *any* book for that matter—for "coercing" you into doing something you didn't want to. That's a crock o' crap, and let us remind you once again, *we don't advocate cheating and all the deception that goes along with it. We're just here to advise those of you who will do it when you have to, when the clock has run out and you just can't afford to get the miserable grade you truly deserve.*

. . . COLLABORATING WITH A BUDDY?

This is where the Code really separates the born cheaters from the posers, those just experimenting with it to be "cool." The born cheater knows that when you go down, you go down alone. The poser tries to weasel out and starts shifting blame around, thereby making the whole situation worse and forever cutting himself off from the Cheating Brotherhood System of Mankind. The Cheating Brotherhood System of Mankind is that inherent quality of both Man and his culture that says, "If we're both getting something out of this shady deal, whatever it may be, then I won't say anything if you don't." For example, you're at the convenience store, buying a twelve-pack. The guy in front of you is getting the same thing. The jittery, zit-faced kid behind the counter mistakenly rings it up for $2.99, about six bucks under the real price, and the other guy doesn't say anything. Now, do you step in and correct the kid so that you and this guy each pay $8.99, or do you wink at the guy when he turns around to leave with a smirk on his face? Gee, that's a tough one.

About nine out of nine times you're going to keep your mouth shut and get the good deal (just don't be winking too much at strange men there, pal), cuz hey, you got it coming to you, don't you? Hell yeah! You've been getting ripped off by these big, billion-dollar, multi-conglomerated, monopolizing, greedy, grubbing, oil-spilling, seal-clubbing, fascist mega-companies for too long, damn it!

Well, at least that's what we all tell ourselves every time we somehow rip *them* off, don't we? Anyway, that, somewhere back there, was the Cheating Brotherhood System of Mankind. You all know it. It goes back to the dawn of Man. Scene: Primitive man, spear in hand, stumbles across a pile of carcasses out in the field left by a not-to-be-seen lion. Fearing another scolding by his berry-gathering wife at home for returning from his hunting duties once again empty-handed, the Homer Simpson–like primitive man looks around for the lion, then starts tugging a carcass to take home, already dreaming of the tall tale he'll get to spin about how he threw down his spear and wrestled this beast one-on-one, making it howl for mercy before he snapped its neck with his bare hands.

Suddenly, though, in the midst of our hero's tugging and daydreaming, another hunter from a different clan walks onto the scene. The two see each other, tense up, and exchange meaningless grunts, each one merely trying to out-grunt the other. Finally the newcomer looks around, sees that the lion is away, and then grabs a carcass for himself, likewise tired of his berry-gathering wife's constant scorn. Through this common act of deviance, they exchange smiles and nicer grunts, until, of course, the lion pops out of nowhere and slaughters these two lazy fools, adding them to his trap-pile of carcasses so he can feed his whole den like a real provider. The moral or the story? Uhhh. . . we don't know. (Is it getting painfully obvious that half the stuff in here is just to amuse you and serves little or no purpose?)

Basically what we've been trying to get at is that if the teacher asks you if so-and-so helped you, you say "absolutely not." Put yourself in that kid's shoes. How would you like it if you showed someone an answer, and then, when they were stupid enough to get caught, *you* got in trouble, too? That sucks!

This whole "Brotherhood" business, though, really comes more into play in the section about plagiarizing, as you will see in the "Paper" section.

. . . USING A CHEATSHEET?

This is an easy one, one we've already alluded to this in book many times over. Quite simply, my friend, YOU EAT IT! EAT! EAT! EAT! Worried about ink on your tongue? The mythical "lead poisoning"? Paper in your logs? Nonsense! The prospects of any of those happening is buried by the prospect of what *does* happen when you get caught cheating.

And what exactly is that? Well, let's just assume the worst-case scenario. Let's say, innocently enough, that you decide to cheat for the first time in your life on this little chemistry test in junior year of high school because you fear that if you don't get at least a B in this class, your straight shot for Harvard is in jeopardy. After all, everyone in your entire family tree, including that thirteen-year-old genius cousin on your mom's side, has gone to Harvard and graduated Summa cum laude. So, seeing no harm, you make a little "Classic" of all the elements and some equations. To make an already-too-long story a little longer: you get caught, don't eat the evidence, and the school's tribunal finds you guilty by reason of stupidity. Checking out your transcript, with that big red "Cheated" stamp across the top of it, your advisor asks if you're any good working with your hands and sends you off to the local vocational/technical school whose commercials on TV you and your friends used to make fun of when you were kids. You can fill in the rest of the story on your own.

Anyway, the bottom line is eat. Eat, eat, eat. Eat the damn evidence and they have absolutely no case. Do so slyly, *as if you're just putting another another piece of gum in your mouth*, à la the great Emmit Fitzhume of *Spies Like Us*. You don't usually look at the teacher to see if he's watching you put a stick of gum in your mouth, do you? No. So don't look at him now either, when he's walking towards you after having caught a glimpse of what he thought was you cheating "or something." It's good to have a real piece of gum in your mouth during the whole test anyway, so that if and when you put this fake piece in, you can say it just combined with the one already in there, you know? Practice the somewhat tricky "swallowing-piece-of-paper-but-not-piece-of-gum-maneuver" (Figure 8-1).

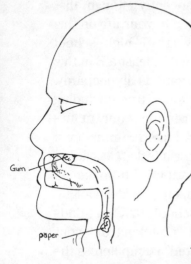

Gum

paper

Figure 8-1

DO NOT, as many people have done, stash the cheatsheet in the test or bluebook or somewhere else like that if the teacher appears to be threatening. Many a teacher has ruffled many a test or bluebook over their head to see if many a thing would fall out, and many a crestfallen student has felt time utterly stop as that damning, incriminating little 2" by 2" piece of paper has fallen slowly and silently before the class, back and forth, and back and forth, spinning slowly over itself, like the first lone leaf of an approaching dismal autumn.

Eat it. We will discuss it no further.

Yup, that should do it. We don't want to spend too much time on the Getting Caught thing because:

A. What to do is usually pretty self-explanatory in most situations.

B. It's mostly all b.s.-ing, which is more of a talent than something which can be taught through a book.

C. The more attention we give it, the more you're apt to think it's ever going to be an issue— which it won't be if you read this whole book, have half a brain, and aren't careless. Really, like most things in life, you'll always be fine unless you get carried away and try to do too much.

D. We're getting sick of talking about tests and want to move on to papers.

E. All of the above.

Chapter 9

Papers Papers Papers

You can make 'em into airplanes, you can pull 'em out from under your windshield wiper and toss 'em half a block, and you can roll 'em into all kinds of fancy "cigarettes," but you just can't write 'em, can you? That is, either you can't or you just never feel like expending all that precious time and mental energy.

Probably about half of you out there in our stellar generation can put a few sentences together without getting a migraine and without having it read like a foreigner's account of his trip to Disneyland. (Like: "Big big mouse wave to me. I scared and look round for help. See only many no-looking-good Americans, very very round, with silly hats on head and 'cheese-dogs' in mouth. Show to wife, we then think very funny. Take many pictures to show friends at home!") The rest of you, unfortunately, can barely write better than that. Blame it on TV, blame it on your schooling system, blame it on Rio, we don't care. The bottom line is that you can't write, and we can't teach you how. Or, you *can* write, but you rarely feel like it unless it's on the bathroom wall or you're trying to impress someone you like with your amazing "Jim Morrison–like" genius. What we *can* teach, however, is how to do little to no real work and get a decent grade on a paper (hopefully). So, first things first.

"PLAGIARISM"

What an ugly, grotesque word. The very sight of it conjures up images of both the bubonic plague and those over-graphic animations of big gray plaque-monsters storming around in toothpaste commercials, doesn't it? Well, at least it does to someone who's been nabbed for it. (So we hear.) If you don't want to become such a person, listen up:

Plagiarism is basically passing off someone else's ideas or words as your own. Some plagiarism is deliberate dishonesty, like, copying material word for word from a book and then submitting it without using quotation marks or documentation as if it were your own paper. But a more common source of plagiarism is simple carelessness—failure to take good notes that use quotation marks, failure to paraphrase words different enough from the original, or failure to get far enough away from the notes in writing the paper.

Now, guess what? That entire paragraph above was plagiarized. Ha ha! Could you tell? Hopefully it was the most boring paragraph in this whole book, and you *could* tell. But most likely, you wouldn't have given it much thought if we didn't point it out. All we did was change a few words—took out a biggie like "sufficiently" here, threw in a dummy such as "like" there, and suddenly it seemed pretty normal.

Before we get ahead of ourselves, though, let's make sure you have a sound grasp of what plagiarism is. No, wait. On second thought, it's probably better if you don't know *exactly* what it is. That way, you'll be better at the primary method of getting out of trouble if busted plagiarizing: Playing Dumb, as discussed later.

All you really need to know from the actual definition is the "word for word" part: You just can *not* do that, son.

GETTING THE MEAT

There are basically three ways for you to get the raw goods for the paper that you will ultimately be handing in "as your own," to use the words of every definition of plagiarism out there. So, without any further ado (and we know there's been a whole lot of ado in this book), here we go.

OLD PAPERS

Old papers float around and linger on campuses and in people's files in far greater abundance than old tests. Everyone seems to cling to their old papers for some reason, most likely as proof that they actually did some academic work at some point in their life. Ask around for old papers and check fraternity and sorority test files. When you score one close enough to your assignment, just photocopy it and promptly give it back to the owner. "No harm done, dude."

Speaking of finding one close to your assignment, it's better to procure old papers early on and *then* choose your paper topics throughout the semester based on the ones you already have.

Also, sometimes you yourself might even have an old paper from a previous class that will work for a current class. Don't hesitate to reuse it.

PROFESSIONAL PAPERS

Every one of you knows that picture in the back of magazines, right in between the "Stop Sweat in Six Weeks" advertisement and the one for those shoes that "Make You Two Inches Taller." Yes, the one of that goofy, stressed-out-looking blond guy in glasses who's propping his head up, and over him it says

"TERM PAPER BLUES?" And every one of you has taken a second glance and thought "Hmmm, maybe some lowly, desperate day."

Well, that lowly day may be here. If so, the actual name of this company is *Research Assistance*, and here are their vital stats:

- ☑ 1-800-351-0222

- ☑ Visa/Mastercard, AMEX or C.O.D.

- ☑ Will Fax papers on the spot

- ☑ 22,000+ papers and growing

- ☑ Rates run about $7.50 per page. Footnote and bibliography pages are included at no extra cost

- ☑ Also does custom papers if needed. More $$

- ☑ Open Mon.– Fri. 9am to 5pm PST. Sat. 11 am to 3 pm

Research Assistance also keeps records of where papers have been ordered from, so make sure the paper you're ordering hasn't already been used at your school.

Here's information for some other term paper places:

CR Research

☑ 1-800-520-PAPERS

☑ Visa/Mastercard, AMEX. No C.O.D., but you can wire $$

☑ Will fax

☑ 5,000+ papers and growing

☑ Rates run about $6–$8 per page

☑ Specializes in rush jobs. Custom papers in 3–12 hrs. More $$

☑ Hours: open 24 hours

Academic Research Group Inc.

☑ 1-800-47RESEARCH, or (201)939-0189

☑ Visa/Mastercard, AMEX, or Money Order

☑ Fax: (201)804-9511

☑ 17,000+ papers

☑ Rates run $7.95 per page

☑ Custom papers $30.00 per page; 7 page minimum

☑ Hours Mon.–Fri. 10 am to 5 pm EST

Electronic Papers

- ☑ 1-800-PAPERS1

- ☑ Visa/Mastercard, AMEX

- ☑ Will Fax

- ☑ Features electronic catalog on disk

- ☑ Rates run $7.00 per page

- ☑ Custom papers $25 per page. Takes 1 week, maximum

- ☑ Hours: Mon.–Fri. 7am–6pm PST. Weekend hours vary

NOTE: When considering buying a paper like this, you should also factor in the rather costly fax-receiving charge at your local copy/fax store.

LOCAL GURUS II

Many campuses today also have "local gurus," as discussed in Chapter 1. These people usually consume five gallons of coffee per day, two packs of cigarettes, and God knows what else as they *crank* (pun intended) out paper after paper on every topic, ranging from "Root Causes of the Ukranian Famine" to "The Role of Market Factors in the Development of Eighteenth-Century Fur Trade" to "Embryonic Rockabilly Polka-dotted Fighter Pilots." Ask around to find these academic hookers, or call all those "tutors" listed in the school paper's classified section and see just how far they take the concept of "tutoring."

DAS BOOK

Here's the gem of this whole chapter, one that very few people have caught on to. *If you can find a book that devotes one nice little small chapter to your paper topic, copy it.* For instance, if you have to do a general paper about the Battle of Shiloh, then just find a book in the library that's about the whole Civil War and has one nice little four-page chapter on the Battle of Shiloh. In such books, chapters are often written like an individual term paper that could stand on its own, complete with a thesis, body, and conclusion.

☑ Remember, book pages like that are usually equivalent to about two school-paper pages (double-spaced, big font, etc.), so a little five-page chapter can turn into ten-page paper rather nicely.

☑ This method should be avoided, though, when your paper assignment deals with subject area in which your teacher is a serious expert. He may have read every book there is on the subject. You never know.

☑ NOTE!!!: As excited as you may be about this idea, VERY IMPORTANT further steps discussed in the following sections must be taken to pull this off, so don't jump the gun just yet there, tiger.

ENSICKLOPEDIA

We've called it "ensicklopedia" because you better be pretty damn sick and pretty damn desperate to resort to copying out of the ol' *World Book* or *Britannica* set in the den. Come on now, copying the encyclopedia? Alright, if you absolutely must, say, because it's the night before the due date, you're in eighth grade, and all the libraries are closed, then follow the steps for "Das Book" maneuver. And *NEVER* list the encyclopedia as one of your sources, in any paper.

THE DOCTOR IS IN: "REWARDING REWORDING"

There's another one for the "say-that-five-times-in-a-row-fast" department. Try it. It quickly turns into something like, "Reerorr-rorr. . . uh, word. . . ing word." Okay, with the wacky and clever intro quickly out of the way, let's talk about the absolute, bottom-line, without a doubt, most important part of plagiarizing papers: Rewording them.

The key to successful plagiarizing is getting the material to look as different from the original source as possible. If you're not plagiarizing the actual words, then you're just plagiarizing the thoughts and ideas—which is mostly just information available in any library.

Any of you who are dumb enough to hand in a paper with the exact language that, say, the *Encyclopedia Britannica* uses *will* get caught and *should* get caught for being so dumb. The only exception to this is for large college classes where you're basically just a faceless, flesh-toned mass with a social security number among a sea of other faceless, flesh-toned masses/social security numbers, and where TA's correct the papers, God love 'em.

For high school and smaller college classes, though, stick to the following guidelines.

Rewording Old Papers. . .

The great thing about old papers from other students is that, more often than not, they're already pretty well dumbed down enough, language-wise, so that you don't have to make many changes.

NOTE: Items in ALL CAPITALS in this part are general rules for rewording any type of paper.

. . . FOR THE SAME TEACHER. . .

☑ If you're handing the paper in to the same teacher who corrected the original version, you've got to make some drastic changes, like the wording of the entire opening paragraph, the conclusion, and any unusual words used throughout it. And always change any word that has an exact synonym that can be used. For instance, change a "because" to a "since," or a "typically" to a "usually," "frequently," "often," etc. *DO AS MUCH AS POSSIBLE TO MAKE YOUR PAPER AS DIFFERENT FROM THE ORIGINAL AS POSSIBLE.* A lot of teachers save copies of every paper they correct.

☑ Make the corrections the teacher has marked on the paper. More importantly, *INSERT MANY NEW STUPID, HARMLESS ERRORS ON YOUR OWN.* The more menial correcting a teacher has to do (spelling, grammar, etc.), the less likely he is to think this paper was manufactured. Distract him; use grammatical errors as a decoy.

☑ Also, when giving a teacher a paper he's already corrected, be careful about including any highly original *conclusions* the writer may have drawn in it: *These are what teachers remember from papers*, not the regurgitation of common facts such as dates and names that they see year in and year out. And by conclusions, we don't just mean the final paragraph; we mean any insightful comments in the paper that appear to have come not from books but from the writer (i.e.,

ones that are not attributed to a source—ones
that aren't footnoted).

☑ Avoid very unusual or specific paper topics. A
professor probably expects to see a unique
paper like "The Launching of the Grateful
Dead's Success Through Jerry Garcia's Role in
the JFK Assassination" only once in his lifetime.

☑ Try to find papers from generic subject areas,
like the Civil War for US history, Freud for psychology, etc.

☑ CHANGE THE DAMN TITLE!

*. . . FOR A DIFFERENT TEACHER AT A SMALL SCHOOL;
OR, ONE AT A LARGE SCHOOL, SAME DEPARTMENT. . .*

A lot of teachers are in cahoots. They know that
papers float around, and, more often than you think,
they confer with each other. Reword it as you would
for the teacher who corrected it last year (or last
month, last week, whatever).

*. . . FOR A DIFFERENT TEACHER AT A LARGE SCHOOL,
DIFFERENT DEPARTMENT. . .*

If you're feeling extremely lazy and know *for a fact*
that two teachers from different departments at a university are not friends *at all*, then you can probably
get away with just changing the title and a few words
here and there (like the opening sentence). Be careful,

though. You never know which oddball teachers are friends with each other. Sometimes opposites attract, like the feminism/lesbian lit. teacher and the football coach/US history teacher or something. Who knew?

. . . *FOR A DIFFERENT SCHOOL ALTOGETHER.*
Well, well, well. In that case, my friend, just follow this sweet little six step program:

1. Boot up the paper on your friend's computer.

2. Go to the title page.

3. Replace their name with yours.

4. Replace the old date with the new one.

5. Press PRINT.

6. Take a big gloating stretch in celebration of the completion of your arduous paper assignment.

Rewording Professional Papers
The big thing you need to know about those ever-enticing professional papers from term-paper hotlines is that they're usually excellent, though occasionally sloppy.

So what, you ask?

The so what is that they are almost always *so* well done and in such thick, high-caliber language that you have to completely rework the whole thing; this often winds up taking just as long as it would've to have just written the paper yourself and saved a hefty chunk of change.

☑ No matter what the case, you certainly can't hand in a paper on fax paper, so plan on spending a good deal of time retyping it, especially those painstaking bibliographies. (Even if you could submit a fax, by the way, the term paper companies have their stamp on the pages, apparently to prevent you from doing so.)

☑ As with rewording any paper, insert plenty of "careless" little errors, change the title, and just generally make it as close to your own writing as possible.

☑ Remember, if you can't even understand the paper, you're sure as hell going to have a hard time putting it into your own words.

☑ Of course, the amount of reworking you have to do depends on the class that the paper is for. Here are some classes where you can hand in a relatively unchanged hotline paper:

- Large college (SS#) classes where there's only one paper

- Assignments in addition to tests that don't involve writing (multiple choice, true/false, etc.)

- Same as above, but with more than one paper assignment. ONLY do this, though, if you can afford to employ hotline papers for *all* the assignments, so that "your writing" is consistent

- Any class if you happen to be a good enough writer so that the teacher wouldn't second-guess a paper where you casually threw around terms like "sub-cognitive anthropomorphizing," or something

- Any class where the teacher is just some blithering, bumbling, drunken old fool

Rewording Book Chapters Into Papers

Go about this in generally the same fashion as you would for rewording other papers, with key emphasis on inserting mistakes, since the book probably won't have any.

Here it is. The important steps we said you needed to know for this baby of a scam. The main thing you need to be concerned with when converting the chapter of a book into a term paper is messing around with the sources listed on your bibliography. Look here:

1. Three-quarters of the books on your bibliography should be nonexistent—in other words, make them up! Create bland, conservative titles for books but unique names for the authors, like

The Civil War, by Cecil Fennington. There are a million books out there called simply *The Civil War*, and as long as you can come up with names more creative than "John Smith," or "Bob Jones," the whole package should slip by unnoticeably realistic. Also, choose a publication date from a long time ago, like the 1940s or 1950s, so that if you have to, you can say the book is out of print and you got your copy at an out-of-town library (when you were on vacation, of course).

2. One-quarter of the books should be genuine. These are to round out the authenticity of the source-lists. Since bibliographies are alphabetized by the authors' last names, make up the names of the fake books so that these, the real books, are mixed in throughout the list for better subliminal effect (if any).

3. *LEAVE THE BOOK YOU ARE COPYING OUT OF OFF ALL LISTS*!!!

4. *FOOTNOTE ONLY FROM THE FAKE BOOKS*!!! By footnoting, all we mean is going through the paper and arbitrarily putting numbers after every few sentences or so.

5. For the corresponding footnote sheet that goes at the end of the paper, just assign to each number the fake books in random order and the fake

page numbers where the given information is supposed to have come from. The page numbers from each book should be close together, since books usually discuss a specific topic for a short series of pages. For example, if three of your footnotes are from Cecil Fennington's *Civil War*, the first one could be from page 257, the second one from 261, and the third from 272.

NOTE: The footnoting maneuver is very tricky. Take your time and set them up right so that the footnote list makes sense as a whole. Coordinate certain sentences you are footnoting with a particular book you've made up so that it appears as if you used one book for one aspect of your research, such as historical facts, and another book for a different aspect of your research, such as personal background.

BUSTED! THE CARDINAL RULES OF PLAGIARIZATION

Getting out of trouble for plagiarizing is a much more difficult and political ordeal than getting out of trouble for cheating on a test. There really isn't much you can say when you've copied another paper and the teacher has it and can just compare them both right on the spot. We've broken up the politics of getting caught plagiarizing into the following, the Cardinal Rules:

1. *PLAY DUMB*. Playing dumb can almost automatically get you out of a first offense if it's the right situation. And by playing dumb, we mean really *play dumb*. Pretend like you had absolutely no idea you were doing anything wrong. "What's plage-er-ize-ing, ma'am?" "Oh, you mean you have to say where you get all the information from? And you can't just copy some of the stuff? I'm sorry. I didn't know that at all. I thought I was just *paraphrasing*, like you said we could. I had no idea. Can I just do it over?" "Paraphrasing" is the key word here: that's when you reword or condense something else into your own words, and it's perfectly legal as long as you're copying factual information and not someone's original ideas. (The problem, though, is that pretty much the only time you get caught straight-up is when you've copied someone else's paper, and no one's going to believe you were dumb enough to think that some student's paper was okay to use as a source in the first place.)

2. *CONTEST IT FOREVER*. Never admit you knew you were doing anything wrong, especially when the teacher doesn't have any real proof but just says "I can tell this writing is not your own." Threaten to keep taking the matter to a higher level, a higher court. Plagiarism is such a tricky,

gray area legally that the cases often go on forever, with both sides unable to fully prove guilt
or innocence. In the big leagues, people sue
each other for publishing books that are too
similar to their own, and yet even if the original
author finally wins the case, he has spent a for-
tune in time, agony, and legal fees. If it's some
friend's paper that the teacher read last year, say
you read it just to get an idea for your paper, but
in no way did you actually copy it or mean to,
though you might have subconsciously used
some of it from memory. By doing this you at
least make the area a little gray.

3. *NEVER IMPLICATE SOMEONE ELSE*. If in fact
   you do go down for the count, do not ever, *ever*
   tell the teacher that your friend gladly gave you
   the paper. Such action is of the highest order of
   uncoolness. You must say that you found it in
   someone's room or your fraternity's files or that
   you just flat-out took it from your friend without
   his knowing. Unless you're ratting out a Mafia
   kingpin, implicating someone else *does not* help
   your cause, though authorities will always tell
   you it will. (See the Naval Academy cheating
   story in Chapter 13.)

4. *LET 'EM FRY*. If someone else who gets busted
   plagiarizing your paper is ever so uncool as to
   say that you gladly gave them the paper, deny

any and all such claims and leave that weasel out to fry. Why should you be implicated? Remember, it does nothing to make his situation better. Say you must've lost the paper somewhere or that the suspect must've taken it from your room.

Chapter 10

Skipping the Reading Process

"These Notes Are Not A Substitute." YEAH, RIGHT!!!

Good ol' little Clifford Hillegrass. Where would we be without "his" notes? Clifford, for those of you who don't know, is the grandfather of educational short-cuts, a true icon in the eyes of those who "just never get around to it," whatever "it" may be.

In young little Clifford's particular case, that "it" was reading books. So, with a pretty good amount of spare cash on his hands, little Clifford would hire English professors from such esteemed institutions of higher learning as the University of Colorado and the University of Nebraska to write in-depth analyses of whatever major literary work he, little Clifford, would have to know for school. As the years and the assignments piled up, little Clifford soon found himself with quite an impressive collection of professional literary synopses and analyses. He had thorough explications of everything from *Huck Finn* to *Hamlet*.

They were all excellent, and friends and school-mates were constantly asking to borrow them. But to make their request seem less mooch-ish, if you will, they would merely ask little Clifford for his "notes."

"Sure," little Clifford would say, not being the brightest pear on the tree, "they're all yours. Just bring 'em back in one piece."

Little Clifford's "notes" became so popular around school that finally one day a friend of his, Ezekiel, said to him, "Hey man, you shelled out a bunch of cash for those things, you should be charging people to use 'em yourself, chump."

And then it all fell into place. Yes. Clifford mass-published all his synopses, slapped a big fancy yellow-and-black cover on each of them, and sold them all over the country as simply "Cliffs Notes," just as all his buddies had always referred to them. The rest, of course, is history. The ironic twist, though? Although now a multimillionaire, poor little Clifford never got a real education, having never read any books, of course. And today, sadly, he can barely even sign his own name, as we've all seen on the inside cover of each and every copy of Cliff's Notes.

Okay. Now, did you believe that story? You did? Really? *Really?* Okay, you didn't. Either way, you shouldn't have, because we just completely made up that whole Paul Harvey–like narrative just for fun, inspired entirely by the ridiculousness of that Clifford Hillygrass signature (Figure 10-1) that's found inside every copy of "his notes." What the hell is that thing? Is that truly the work of a grown man? If so, then our

Figure 10-1

version of how Cliff's Notes evolved must be true (and we believe that it is). Look at that thing! It looks like a signature from somebody's first bank book or something, like the one you get when you're five years old just to learn how the banking process works, you know? Geez, Cliff, seeing as how you hired somebody else to read the books, write the summaries, write the analyses, and probably even write the introduction that you sign, you should've just gone the whole nine yards and hired somebody to write your own damn name for you as well!

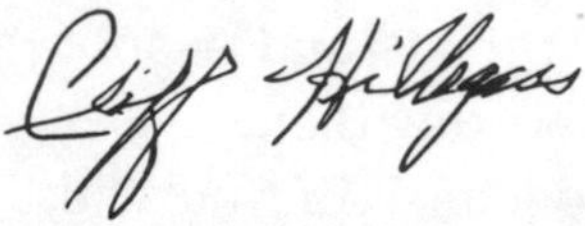

Seriously, though, Clifford Hillsgrass (if our deciphering of the spelling is correct) has indeed done our generation a great service/disservice. Before we go any further, though, this would probably be a good time to lump Monarch Notes in with Cliff's. Very briefly, they are exactly the same, the only difference being the slightly stealthier red covers of the Monarchs as opposed to the loud, construction-sign coating of Cliff's. (We've even had to add the possessive apostrophe that poor illiterate Clifford forgot altogether.) But for convenience's sake, from this point on we will refer to any and all such aids as CliffNotes, because:

A. no one ever refers to them as Monarchs

B. no one ever says "Cliff's Notes," they just say "CliffNotes," as in "Hey, did ya get that CliffNotes, man?"

Now, on one hand, the service CliffNotes has done our generation is that we never have to read those cumbersome, time-consuming, pain-in-the-ass books for class. The disservice, on the other hand, is that you can't relate anything in a conversation these days to a great character like Oliver Twist or Jay Gatsby, but only to characters like "Kramer," or "Norm." Oh yeah, and we're also going to be the most elitterate, unsucksesfull genaration in american histry. That kind of sucks too. (Unless, of course, you can make money writing books exploiting and perpetuating certain dimensions of our underachievement! Yeeeee hawww! God Bless America!)

So, as out of line with the rest our preachings as this may seem, we really do encourage you to read the actual books as much as you can. It really is the best way to improve and expand your mind, and it really does pay off. If nothing else, it's just a good feeling to totally know what someone's talking about when they allude to something from fiction. At the *very* least, you'll get a few *Jeopardy!* questions right. But we know, it's not necessarily that you never *want* to read the books, it's usually just that you can't keep up with the hundred-pages-per-night assignments of the teacher, and as soon as you fall behind you're never going to catch up in time, so why even bother? Right?

Anyway, the only way *we're* going to keep your attention is to keep breaking everything up into big, easy-to-read, bold-headed sections. So, here we go. . .

USING, ABUSING, AND UNUSING CLIFFNOTES

Sometimes you need 'em, sometimes you don't.

Camouflaging Them

The first thing you must do when obtaining any set of CliffNotes is tear off the cover. That's right, rip that screaming-to-be-noticed-by-teachers yellow-and-black cover right off. We wonder, did Señor Hildegrass (or whatever the hell his name is) cut some deal with educational authorities to come with up the absolute loudest, most attention-getting cover possible? It's like some kind of flashing yellow sign you'd expect to find at a hairpin curve on the back of an icy mountain road. Well, even if Mr. Hildegard did cut a deal like that, he must not have really had his heart in it, because the covers come off easier than an Under 21 stamp. So do it. Tear it off. You never know when one of those things could fall out of your bag at the wrong time.

Abusage I: Plagiarizing
There are only two types of teachers who even look at CliffNotes.

One kind is a newer breed of teachers who are so baked half the time that they don't remember half the stuff they learned in college. These guys probably wouldn't even care if you plagiarized; they're just teaching in the meantime while they write the Great American Drivel—er, "novel," rather.

The other kind is the prick who keeps them handy to make sure his students' amazing new insights aren't coming pre-packaged in this cozy yellow-and-black wrapping. Guys like this do exist somewhere out there, but only in rare cases, so don't worry about using ideas from the CliffNotes in your papers. You can plagiarize some lines, or even whole pararaphs sometimes, as long as the writing isn't greatly superior to your own. Any teacher would likely catch on to some foul play if a paper went something like, "Hamlet is, like, this pissed-off guy, because, like, his mom's shacking with his uncle, who just murdered his dad and all. So, like, Oedipal manifestation within dialoguean Hamlet contrasts starkly with the active Hamlet, and yet altogether is not completely unmasked by his rather primordial—albeit mundane—adoration for the young Ophelia. Like, get it, Mr. Hand?"

Abusage II

For open-book, in-class essays about books you haven't read, just strip down the CliffNotes to their bare essentials and tape what you need inside the actual book (Figure 10-2). The only problem with this method, though, is that if a suspicious teacher comes over to inspect your book, you're screwed.

You certainly can't eat a set of CliffNotes, now can you?

Figure 10-2

Unusage

Every time you come across an insurmountable reading assignment, you don't necessarily need to rush out and buy the CliffNotes. Don't worry, we're not going to annoy you with the "joys of reading" again. We just want to point out the universally overlooked fact that many novels have adequate summaries of themselves RIGHT IN THE INTRODUCTION. Almost every classic has some kind of foreword or introduction that all students automatically skip over on their way to see that "Sweet! This book starts on page nineteen, dude!" Yes, well, that's usually a hollow victory, because those first eighteen pages usually contain just about everything you need to know to get through a class discussion of the book. *INTRODUCTIONS ARE USUALLY EXCELLENT IN-DEPTH ANALYTICAL ESSAYS ABOUT THE TEXT, SUMMARIZING THE WHOLE THING ALONG THE WAY.*

Unusage II

Let's face it: Sometimes you don't even have time to read the CliffNotes. Those things can be over a hundred pages long! In that case, go to a much broader source that covers tons of different books. For instance, sometimes you can just look up a book up in the encyclopedia and find all the information you need to get through a class discussion or two. There are also things like Shakespeare Encyclopedias, in which one big book you'll find everything from two-sentence definitions of *"S'wounds"* to one- to two page (cncyclo-size) summaries of entire plays that you can read in five minutes!

The main point here: there are many other easily accessible summaries of books other than CliffNotes, so don't panic if you can't get them. It takes ten minutes in the school library to dig up some kind of summary you can read so that WHEN THE TEACHER ASKS YOU A QUESTION IN CLASS, HE WON'T KNOW YOU HAVEN'T READ A WORD. Then, of course, there is always. . .

THE MOVIE VERSION!

Oh! How sweet it is to find out that a book you are supposed to read is available in the much more entertaining and stress-free movie form! There's a movie version of just about every classic, but be careful. They are really condensed, and you typically wind up learning only the most basic workings of the plot and a few things about the two main characters. Quizzes usually ask you all kinds of junk about subordinate characters and subplots.

And even if watch the movie inside and out, ALWAYS AT LEAST LOOK THROUGH THE ACTUAL BOOK AS WELL. Sometimes a movie can be an excellent adaptation of the book, but the teacher might ask you something really basic about how the book is formulated that you wouldn't know from the movie alone. For example, if your teacher asked you how the book *The Color Purple* is set up, you wouldn't know just from watching the movie that it consists of a series of letters "written by" the main character to God, most beginning with "Dear God." One simple glance at a few random pages and you would know this.

COMBO

A really solid way to get a quick working knowledge of a book is to read a summary while watching the movie. This way, those flat, faceless descriptions of the characters in the summaries come to life. If you can picture them in your mind, you're a lot more likely to be able to discuss them in class.

Chapter 11

Miscellaneous
Ass-ignments

In this section, we're going to tackle all those extra oddball assignments every student has to do a few times during their academic career under the tutelage of some ass of a teacher. Thus, we'll call them Ass-ignments. We'll cut right to the chase, and you'll know exactly what we're talking about.

JOURNALS

Good God, man, now just how the hell did this raw deal get started? Doesn't this sound like kind of a sick idea, when you really think about? You got a grown man or woman heading a class of innocent young adolescents, and out of nowhere that man or woman suddenly decides that they want to read twenty young, personal diaries every week! What kind of sickos are these people? Forcing nervous, hormonally insecure kids to spill their beans on paper every day so that they, the teachers, can get their rocks off? Someone should put an end to this filth! to this extortion of privacy! to this modern day mental molestation!

Yes, they should. But until they do, you're still gonna have to produce a couple of bogus diaries sometime under the guise of their being "journals." What's the difference? Nothing. It's just a more politically correct term a grown man can use to solicit your diary. In light of this crap, we unreservedly say *SCREW 'EM!!!*

These people don't have any right to know what's really going on in your head if you don't want to share it with them. So, take advantage of these assignments to work on the ol' creative writing skills! That's right, feel no guilt making up all kinds of nonsense in your "journal." They can't do anything about it. It's your life, it's your business.

Journals are usually graded simply pass or fail, so just do enough to pass. Anyway, here are a couple things to remember.

Color-Code It

If you are filling out the whole thing from start to finish the day before it's due, REMEMBER TO USE AT LEAST FOUR DIFFERENT COLORED WRITING

IMPLEMENTS: #2 PENCIL, BLACK PEN, BLUE PEN, #3 PENCIL, OR RED PEN, GREEN PEN, ETC.

Even the flakiest of teachers will give you a hard time at the very least if you hand in sixty different journal entries from sixty supposedly different days all written in what would have to be some magically unloseable WonderPen.

"If You Can't Tell That It Sucks, You Must Pass"
Doesn't have quite the ring to it as "Doesn't fit, must acquit," but we don't really care all that much at this point. Basically, if you're just writing a bunch of complete crap, make it illegible. Go ahead and let your pen do the wandering as you rattle off the sloppiest writing since Clifford K. Hillegrass's "signature." Like we told you back in Chapter 7, *they can't flunk it if they can't read it.*

A good sentence to make legible, though, would be something like, "Man, now that I look back at what I've written, I can't believe how sloppy my handwriting is. I'm taking my time writing this right now, but this sucks, it's taking forever and it's driving me crazy, so screw it." Then, switch back to sloppy mode. Make it look like you can't help but write sloppily, like your mental sanctity depends on it.

Come to think of it, while you're making stuff up anyway, you might as well go ahead and play with the teacher's mind and write random stuff like "Police haven't found the body yet, thank God," or "I can't believe one of my other teachers keeps offering me money to do all those nasty things to me." Go ahead, arouse some suspicion, create an awkward scene for somebody else, and get a kick out of it. After all, it's not like you *volunteered* to share your thoughts, now is it?

LABS

The Worst. Those seem to be the only two words we can think of when we remember labs: *The Worst*. Anyway you look at it, labs are simply the worst part of the whole educational process. Whether they are for a science class or an anthropology class or a computer class or whatever, they suck because:

A. Labs are usually an additional non-credit hour out of your time per week *on top* of the regular class time, and they are always held at some ungodly hour, like either at the crack of dawn or at five o'clock on Friday afternoon.

B. When you're at lab, you're forced to perform taxing, difficult tasks under the tight supervision of the fanatical teacher or some gung-ho TA. And we're talking about such fun tasks as gutting a smelly pig fetus or programming a computer so it can print your name across the screen a million times at the touch of button. Yippee.

C. Labs usually count as a ridiculous amount of your grade for the semester, like forty percent or something.

D. Labs just flat out suck all around, and that's all there is to it.

E. All of the above.

F. And then some.

Okay, now that we've sufficiently established the fact that labs suck, let's discuss a few things that can make them suck slightly less.

SuperPartner!

Yes, if you don't mind compromising your godlike image one hour per week, ditch partnering with your buddy for labs and go straight for the nerdy little brainchild in the corner who would be thrilled to have you as a new friend. If you score a SuperPartner, show some concern at first during the labs, but keep screwing up so that your partner takes over. From then on, you're in copy heaven. Just keep being nice, *including* out in the hallways and stuff.

"Just confirming"

If you do wind up with a partner who's as much of slapdick as you are, you should take turns alternately spending a good deal of the lab time snooping around looking at other people's results under the facade of "Hey, we got 112 for number four, what'd you guys get?" Then when you're over there to supposedly look at number four, snake as many answers as you can off their page with your free eye.

Special Ed
Often when you're completely clueless during a lab, the TA will pretty much just steer you through it, i.e., do it for you. So, if you can handle asking a lot of stupid questions and having one random person—a TA, no less—think you're a moron, go for it. It beats doing it yourself.

"Makeup" labs
This is for when there are several different TA lab instructors for the course and you're pretty sure the one you have isn't that tight with the teacher. In this case, just copy all the labs you missed at the end of the semester from someone who's already gotten theirs corrected, and then hand them all in at once to the main teacher and say you did them in makeup with Dung or whoever. (Foreign-exchange TA's like Dung are best because of the language barrier, should the teacher question him.) You'll probably need to forge Dung's signature or initials or whatever on all these "made-up" labs, so learn what that hieroglyphic looks like.

EXTRA CREDIT

Extra credit exists in this world because of two very different, polar opposite types of people. One is the geeks, who just aren't satisfied with the curriculum and feel compelled to do more work on their own. (!) The other is the rest of us, who so frequently fall on the brink of getting lousy grades that compassionate teachers wind up giving us an opportunity to do extra credit work so that:

A. we don't get ourselves in trouble with bad grades.

B. *they* don't get themselves in trouble by turning in class rosters full of C's and D's.

Sometimes we don't even have a choice about whether we want to do some extra credit or not because it's either do it or get the F that your test scores add up to. So. . .

EXTRA CREDIT THIS!

Extra credit is easy to forge and get away with because no one really cares all that much about it; they just like to see the fact that you did it. With this in mind, chalk up the extra-credit points with a bunch of bogus work. Each class has its own random type of extra credit, so it's hard for us to advise you on how to forge it. But most of the time it just involves showing up at some kind of deal outside class, signing in, and grabbing some of the sheets to fill out and hand in.

The key is to just make an appearance and/or hand in the sheets every week, whether or not you actually do anything at all. Just find out from someone the basic gist of what you need to write about, and do it. Remember: Teachers and TA's have a lot of *real* work to correct, and more often than not they are just going to glance at these picayune little assignments and mark off a check next to your name in the gradebook.

This typical apathy on their part means you can also copy your friends stuff as much as you want, and you hardly have to worry about changing it at all.

TWO FOR ONE

Here's a great way to kill two birds with one BB pellet: If you have to do community service work for some reason (like some legal or school judiciary reason), look around and try to find an activity that you can also get extra credit for in one of your classes. For instance, if you're in a psychology class, opt for the mental hospital community service deal instead of the old-age home one or whatever.

Just don't tell the teacher you did it for community service. Make the teacher think you *care*. Yeah right. That's a laugh. But they'll still eat it up.

Chapter 12

Legends of the Mall

Surely when you saw this book sitting there on the bookstand, gleaming new, its binding uncracked like so many of your textbooks, and calling out to you "buy me! buy me!", you smiled to yourself for a moment as your thoughts drifted back to some of your own minor cheating accomplishments and then on to those of that one infamous slapdick from your high school, that one smirking, conniving b.s.-er who thrived on cheating and always got away with it, who never studied a night in his life and made better grades than most everyone else, who took cheating as a passion and did it for the mere sport of it sometimes, trying only to outdo his previous feats. And when he graduated, when he stepped up to the podium and received that purely hollow degree, that fraudulent piece of paper, a smiling but slightly uneasy applause rippled through the audience.

For while his parents clapped proudly, those who knew of his antics wondered if he planned on abusing the system at college as well. And, what's more, would he ever stop? Would this pattern of cheating sadly turn to the use of aliases, tax fraud, and the like someday? How long before he made the Senate? No one was quite sure, but no one really worried about it either. Because, deep down, everyone knew he would get away with probably just about anything, and that soon thereafter, he would never be heard from again. He would remain only in the tales of admiring underclassmen, who would recount his feats and exaggerate them just enough to make him immortal, to make him a god to all up-and-coming cheaters, to make him. . . legend.

This character has shown his face in fiction in varying forms, from the charismatic Mike Seaver of *Growing Pains*, to the seasoned veteran Emmit Fitzhume of *Spies Like Us*, to the promising young prodigy Bartholomew J. Simpson of *The Simpsons*. And however you know him from your own experience, just apply that guy's face to the following tall and true cheating tales. We could only gather a few, and we're sure many of you out there know (or have done) some doozies, so again, as we told you in the introduction, send 'em on in for our followup book, *The Cheater's Handbook's Extra Credit: Ideas From Our Readers*.

FROM ONE SCHMUCK TO ANOTHER

We'll start with a cute little tale from someone deeply involved with the production of this book (eh em). This person, who shall remain nameless, was in a large class that was broken up into four sections headed by four different teachers. The hundred-student-plus class met once a week as a whole, twice a week in four separate rooms of twenty-five or so. The whole class had to take the same tests and write the same papers, and each of the four discussion leaders corrected his section's stuff on his own.

Toward the end of the semester, having missed over a solid month of class and yet knowing that the discussion leader neither noticed, cared, nor took off points for late papers, I—whoops! We mean, uh, *this student*, rather—waited for one of the more on-the-ball discussion leaders to hand back his section's papers and leave them outside his door to be picked up by his students. Knowing not only that the two different professors were swamped with work at this hectic time of year, but also that they were not friends *at all*, the student went to the other professor's office when he wasn't there, grabbed the highest-graded paper out of the box by the door, walked down the hall, photocopied it, and then stuck it back in the box just where he had found it—all within two minutes. He then went home and, being extremely lazy at that point in his life, retyped it *word for word*, the only change being his name and social security number at the top. He handed it in, and though it was late, received the same grade that the original author had gotten: A.

INSIDE SOURCE

One freshman student fell upon what he originally thought was the misfortune of working at his university's printing shop, where teachers have their non-published textbooks and/or collections of certain handouts printed and bound. Then one fateful day as he was in the back working on something, a teacher of his dropped off the next day's test to be mass copied. The tests were copied by an adult employee and then boxed up and sealed. The student eyed the precious cardboard box and began salivating. The tests are in there, he thought, right in *there*. The temptation was too much, so when no one else was around he slit the box open along the tape ever so slightly, pulled out a copy of the test, and then taped the box back up perfectly. The teacher had hundreds of students, so he'd never notice one missing test form. The student then made a couple photocopies of the test to pass along to his friends—purposely omitting, though, one of the pages, so that he would be the only one to know *all* the answers and thus get a, yup, you guessed it, a 98. He did the same thing for every test and finished with a perfect 98.5 average. (He splurged and gave himself a 100 on the final.)

HEY, AT LEAST HE
WASN'T DEALING DRUGS

One brilliantly devious student took advantage of today's technology and the fact that his professor had the answers to each multiple-choice test posted outside his office *during* the test. The professor did this, apparently, so that students with the problems fresh on their minds could go and check the answers directly after the test to see how well they did. The student, knowing after the first test that the answers were posted in black and white just a couple of buildings away during the test, devised a way to get those answers during the test. First, he purchased a pager/beeper that vibrated instead of beeping to let you know there was a message. Then, he would have a friend of his go to the professor's office during the test, write down all the answers, walk down the hall, pick up the pay phone, and call the pager. The pager would vibrate, signaling that the answers were coming in. The test-taker would look down and read the answers from the code he had established with his friend! The number 1 meant answer A, 2 meant B, 3 meant C, and 4 meant D. He got hundreds on the rest of the tests. Pretty sweet, huh?

Chapter 13

So Close! But No Cigar: They Had Greatness Within Their Grasp

This section is dedicated not to the common fool who copies even the essay portion of a test off the adjacent nerd and consequently gets laughed out of school by the disciplinary board. No. This is for those who fell just short of achieving greatness, those who had a brilliant plan but let it all slip away at the last second because of either overconfidence or simple carelessness. It's like every criminal mastermind from all those movies—the James Bond flicks, the *Die Hard*s, the *Fletch*'s. Each of those criminal masterminds has some veritably ingenious plan to steal two billion dollars or erase the world's economy or nuke the entire free world or something, but inevitably their own hubris opens up a loophole just tiny enough for the hero to foil the plot. We've all seen it a million times. And even the most seasoned of us cheaters have fallen prey at some point to our own hubris and the carelessness that goes along with it. Take for example, the following story, which did indeed happen to yours truly, the author, midway through junior year.

A MATTER OF MILLIGRAMS

Not prepared at all for a physics test one Monday, I decided to make a nice little three-day weekend out of the whole thing and stayed home, enjoying the fruits of game shows, Nintendo, and Doritos. That Monday night, I was still too lazy to even call anyone and find out just what exactly was on this test that I would be making up the next day when I was "recuperated from my terrible illness," of course. So, the next day, there I am, sitting all alone in a room taking this bitch of a test, which, conveniently enough, consisted of a stack of dittos. (If you've read this book carefully up to this point, you should be able to guess where I'm going with this.) Not knowing a single thing on one of the pages, I panicked. Then, when I looked down and saw that the whole page was worth twenty-five points, it hit me. Just rip it out and say you never got it. Yes! What an ingenious idea!

So I did. Then, being the foolish young sixteen-year-old that I was, I went up to the teacher at the end of the hour (she had me taking it next door while class was going on) and said, "Here you go. Was there a page missing, though? It jumps from question fifteen on this page here to question twenty-one on this page here." "Oh!" she said. "I'm sorry, I must've messed up when I was making it and left off that page. Can you finish it right now?"

I looked at the clock and said, "Uh, no, actually. I'm late for my next class. I can come by and take it after lunch."

She said that was cool, so I left, walked down to the student lounge, went over the "nerd-corner" of the lounge, and had some nerd fill out the page I had swiped. I memorized the answer and the work that led up to it.

After a carefree lunch in which I got to brag about my exploits endlessly, I sashayed on back to the physics room, and, like Bart Simpson in the episode where he pulls a similar stunt, I nonchalantly jotted down the answers I had memorized, and then handed in the page.

"This is terrible," said my teacher. "I. . . I can't believe you did this. I'm so disappointed in you. I'm so. . . I'm so *hurt.*"

"What?" I asked, innocently. She pointed to the question, then to my work. My heart dropped like a ton of feathers.

"You used the old number, for crying out loud! I changed it. I changed it!"

She did. Just barely, but she did. She changed the problem. In one of the problems the number I used for the weight of an object was 5.1 grams, just like what I had memorized. On the makeup sheet the number was now 5.15 grams. That is, if you looked *really* carefully. She had added that stinking little .05 of a stinking gram in with a stinking little pencil, the stinking little. . . Nah, I guess I can't really say anything bad about her. She outfoxed me. It's as simple as that. She won.

Needless to say, I got in trouble. And though she may have won that battle, I kind of won the war. Through much plea bargaining, b.s.ing, and ass-kissing, it didn't go on my permanent record. Phew! Wouldn't want anyone to know about that one!

DON'T MESS WITH ETS

Following is a horror story scarier than anything Stephen King could concoct.

Problem #1

Scenario: A student scores a 620 on his first SAT attempt, so he takes the Princeton Review's intensive six-week preparation course. He then scores a 1030 on his second SAT attempt. But the test's publisher, Educational Testing Service, nullifies this second score, declaring that the improvement is too great and the student must've had someone else take the test for him.

Question: The outraged student and his family then prove his innocence by which one (or more) of the following?

A. Proposing that he take a polygraph lie detector test.

B. Proposing that a fingerprint specialist examine his answer sheets.

C. Hiring a handwriting expert who verifies that the signature on the answer sheet is in fact that of the accused student.

D. Visiting the school where the student took the SAT, and having him identify his test proctor out of a lineup. In turn, the proctor confirms that the accused student had indeed taken the test in her classroom.

E. All of the above.

F. None of the above.

Answer: E *and* F. The student's family did all of the above, but to no avail.

The Bill Gates of scantron sheets, almighty ETS controls testing in every field from shopping center

management to manicuring(!), and in over 170 coun-
tries. A gargantuan corporation, ETS has crushed
more than thirty court challenges to its authority as
final arbiter of scores on the SATs, which account for
forty percent of ETS's hundreds of millions of dollars
in revenues each year. ETS maintains that if they
entertain such challenges to their totalitarian test-
tallying, "protracted trials will become the customary
means of resolving. . . disputes." Hey, anyone heard of
America?

What a crock of crumbled cookies. Sure, this kid's
score went up a whopping 410 points, but to what?
1030? Big deal. No offense, but the whopping factor
stops there. It's not like Harvard and MIT were batter-
ing his doors down after that median level score. But
from 620 to 1430? Now *that* would be whopping.

Take it from a graduate of the Princeton Review:
those classes work. I personally went up two hundred
points, but I was starting a little higher than the dude
in question. He started in much more of a swing zone
('tween 600 and 1000), where there's more room for
vast improvement through the many great tactics that
courses offered by the Princeton Review and Stanley
Kaplan teach.

So I don't think he cheated, but obviously it doesn't
matter what I think, or what his proctor thinks, or his
parents, or even his parochial school teachers. (Cler-
gymen, for Christ's sake!) All that matters is that ETS
has a much bigger legal fund than you do, so don't

mess with 'em. Unless, of course, it's to make fun of the fact that they seriously administer manicuring exams, like. . .

Problem #2

The part of the hand that should be directed toward ETS is which of the following?

A. the cuticle

B. a hangnail

C. the middle finger!

SINK OR SWIM

Probably the biggest cheating scandal in American history began on December 11, 1992, when a civilian who worked in the copying center of the United States Naval Academy in Annapolis, Maryland, sold a copy of the notoriously difficult electrical engineering final exam to a midshipman for a reported $5,000. The copy floated around the tightly knit campus like pollen, and the cheating scandal was soon born. Everyone did so well that school officials caught on. Ultimately, 133 midshipmen were implicated in the crime. Some spilled the beans, some zipped their lips, and everyone was a nervous wreck. With all the fingerpointing, lying, and potential career-ruining punishment at hand, the Class of 1994 was torn apart over the next year as government officials grilled anybody and everybody on campus about who did what.

The Navy holds honor as its highest virtue. To give you an idea of just how much, consider this: A midshipmen responsible for a horrible drunk-driving accident was given demerits, while a female midshipman who reported her weight as six pounds less than her true weight was *expelled*. You cannot lie or cheat in the Navy. Period.

After an exhaustive investigation, twenty-four midshipmen were expelled, sixty-four were severely punished, and the United States Navy was forever shamed. Most of the twenty-four expelled were ones who came forward and admitted to cheating. They thought confessing would save them from expulsion like the investigators told them it would. So after a lifetime of hard work to get into one of the nation's top military schools, after a lifetime of dreaming of success in the Navy and working for it, in the hope of one day becoming a captain, or a general, or an admiral, they were thrown out on their asses onto the hard cement, out into a world where no one was ever going to hire them or respect them ever again. As for the rest of the alleged cheaters?

They lied.

That's right, the ones who never, ever admitted a word to anybody graduated without so much as a blemish on their transcripts.

The lessons to be learned here? We hope they're quite obvious by this point.

1. NEVER, EVER ADMIT TO CHEATING!!! EVER!!! Our very own government shows us why!

2. NEVER, EVER HELP CIRCULATE AN ACTUAL TEST THE NIGHT BEFORE IF YOU GET YOUR HANDS ON ONE, as discussed in Chapter 1. That's it. Case closed.

Chapter
14

Farewell, Good Luck, and Don't Be Stupid

Well, that should just about do it, partner. Hope this book has been informative without really encouraging cheating. Seriously, try to learn as much as you possibly can. I cannot even begin to tell you how glad you will be to know stuff out in the real world when you're constantly confronted by idiotic people making idiotic claims in idiotic ways every time you're attempting to deal with something, whether it's at work, at the family gathering, or at a bar. Knowledge is power. It really is. And the best part? It's free. So get as much as you can.

Unfortunately, though, we don't live in a world that necessarily rewards knowledge. Our world tends to reward production first and foremost. And as the population grows larger and our uniqueness in that population grows smaller, efficient ways of sorting through all the faceless names become more important. In the process, those ways become more cold.

Soon after birth we are given social security numbers the way television sets are given serial codes, and the thing that is going to get us from one stage of life to the next is the figures next to that column with our names and serial codes in it. In the career world, those figures may indicate to someone how many cars you sold, or how much productivity increased at the plant you supervise, or how many prosecution trials you have won. But in order to even get to that point, we all must go to school first. And the things that get us from one level to the next in school is really the same thing: Numbers, only except they're called "grades." Whatever.

The point here is that in this endless cycle of producing higher numbers in order to reach so-called higher places, other things often get swept by the wayside. In law, for instance, a defense attorney may have been more concerned with winning his case than the fact that his client is a cold-blooded murderer who will strike again. In car sales, the salesman obviously cares more about getting his commission than the fact that this used car might break down in a month. And, sadly enough, in school, your grades greatly determine your next school.

So who can blame us for feeling pressure to get better grades than we might truly deserve? Who really cares if we know a B's worth of material but want that A's worth of recognition so that we can get into the better school, the better job? People cut corners everywhere, in every facet of business, and as long as our world is set up to reward numbers, none of us should be too quick to judge those who do whatever it takes to get those numbers. This is our system, and each and every one of us is part of the problem because we all do the same thing. "How much does so-and-so make?" "How many times have you been to such-and-such island?" "How many square feet is this?" Etc.

All this is not even to say that our system is flawed or anything. No. This is just to say that certain allowances must be made. Everyone runs out of time sometimes. Everyone screws up sometimes. And everyone wants to make it to the next highest level, whatever that may be. So I defy any of you out there reading this, fan or foe, mischievous student or scornful professor, to delve deep back into your expansive experiences in this life you have lead and not find at least one time in which you cut a corner, or sneaked a peek, or looked the other way, or just simply wished there were something you could do to better the situation you were in at that time.

Don't kid yourself. Any of you. Everyone does some sketchy things sometimes. And sometimes, because of poorly managed time and because of a system that rather coldly rewards numbers above all else—YOU JUST GOTTA CHEAT, BROTHA!

So do it if you have to. Cheat. Big deal. And refer to this handbook in those situations. Just don't think it's "cool" to cheat and go out of your way to do so when you'd do perfectly fine on your own. Please. That's something I did way too much of, and as a result I'm now at a loss whenever a hot debate about America's history comes up, and my ignorance drives me crazy.

Anyway. That'll be all for now. Hope to hear from you for our imminent sequel *The Cheater's Handbook's Extra Credit: Ideas From Our Readers*. You can reach me care of ReganBooks, 10 E. 53rd Street, New York, NY 10022. Thanks, and don't get caught with this puppy in your bag, Einstein.

INDEX

ABOUT THE AUTHOR

BOB CORBETT has pulled off numerous and wildly ambitious cheating scams, including stealing a semester's worth of credits from his university and paying someone to ace his AP tests. Because he didn't do too much studying, he now has to write books like this one to make a living.